Redwan Ahmed is a BA (Hons) Economics graduate, author of two poetry books (*Stories He Couldn't Tell* and *Psychological Sunrises & Sunsets*), currently working in the Civil Service for the Ministry of Defence.

Despite Redwan's degree (Third Class Honours), he did not hold back in seeking opportunities which would challenge him further. In fact, he found his passion in a career in the Civil Service.

He has shown his willingness to drive social mobility for the less disadvantaged in the BAME community through Careers Pal, an initiative to drive students and graduates in the right direction with their careers.

Redwan Ahmed

CIVIL SERVICE TACTICAL STRATEGIES

> Hello, student/graduate/job hunter, it's me, the author!
> I hope you'll enjoy reading this book as much as I enjoyed writing it. Please note this is the original copy, therefore I am aware the text in the visuals may not be as clear. A final copy will be available on Amazon, so do feel free to direct message me on Instagram **(@careerspal)** for clearer visuals. However, I do hope every chapter in this book helps you reach your career ambitions. I wish you every success in job hunting and finding a career that's worthwhile and impactful. You can check out my other books, although they are poetry.
> ~ Redwan Ahmed

AUSTIN MACAULEY PUBLISHERS™
LONDON • CAMBRIDGE • NEW YORK • SHARJAH

Copyright © Redwan Ahmed 2024

The right of Redwan Ahmed to be identified as author of this work has been asserted by the author in accordance with sections 77 and 78 of the Copyright, Designs and Patents Act 1988.

All rights reserved. No part of this publication may be reproduced, stored in a retrieval system, or transmitted in any form or by any means, electronic, mechanical, photocopying, recording, or otherwise, without the prior permission of the publishers.

Any person who commits any unauthorised act in relation to this publication may be liable to criminal prosecution and civil claims for damages.

A CIP catalogue record for this title is available from the British Library.

ISBN 9781035849222 (Paperback)
ISBN 9781035849239 (ePub e-book)

www.austinmacauley.com

First Published 2024
Austin Macauley Publishers Ltd®
1 Canada Square
Canary Wharf
London
E14 5AA

I will start by saying 'Bismillah' which translates to 'In the Name of Allah (God)'.

My motivation for writing this book has stemmed from having insightful conversations with amazing connections I made on LinkedIn and throughout my poetry journey.

I would like to acknowledge my best friend, Ayshhh, who used to be my client when delivering career sessions through Careers Pal and now considered my favourite motivator. She's the only one who's been able to see the vision through this and understand how valuable this book will be for the many.

I would also like to thank the civil servants who contributed towards the 'Pros of Working for the Civil Service' chapter by sharing their perspectives on what they felt were pros of working for the civil service in their rightful opinion (pen names have been used).

Table of Contents

Abstract	**9**
Chapter 1: Personal Challenges Faced Before Applying for the Civil Service	**11**
Chapter 2: Remedies to Imposter Syndrome at the Time of Applying	**18**
Chapter 3: Civil Service Graded Structure	**22**
Chapter 4: Civil Service Application Process Cycles (Traditional Route Vs Fast Stream Route)	**25**
Chapter 5: Transferable Experiences Required for Civil Service Roles	**29**
Chapter 6: Pros of Working For The Civil Service	**38**
Chapter 7: Behaviours Structure & Analysis (AO-SEO Levels)	**44**
Chapter 8: Personal Statement Structure & Analysis (EO-SEO Levels)	**62**
Chapter 9: Ace Any Civil Service Interview (Face-To-Face, Pre-Recorded, Virtual)	**72**
Concluding Remarks	**105**
References	**108**

Abstract

Civil Service has been the pinnacle of government. In fact, many aspire to become Diplomats for a country they have pride and passion for or would like to know what it is like working at the heart of government and shaping the policies that have a profound impact on the wider society. This book is intended to serve the educational purpose of helping students, graduates, and career consultants conceptualise the process of applying to the UK Civil Service from start to finish and apply strategies that will drive their success in every stage of the Civil Service recruitment process. This, in no way, is classed as an **OFFICIAL** guidance for Civil Service. It is merely from my outlook working in the UK Civil Service for a good couple of years now.

Gems You Will Discover From Reading This Book:

- Insider section, which explores how a student is faced with personal challenges, picks himself up, keeps on going, and makes a realistic transition from Graduate to Civil Servant and Career Coach.
- Experience the effects of Imposter Syndrome and how you can find your very own antidote to repel the long-lasting effects on your Mental Health.
- Understand the Graded Structure that Civil Service follows from the bottom grade (Administrative Officer) to the senior grade (Grade 7).
- Learn how any experience you hold is transferable in the Civil Service through a compelling first-person narrative.

Chapter 1: Personal Challenges Faced Before Applying for the Civil Service

Before I go into the personal challenges I faced before applying for the Civil Service, I thought it'd be good for you to understand my journey leading to applying in the first place.

I will rewind to 2008–2010, when I was studying for my GCSEs. In my school, a Careers Advisor attended the prestigious Career Service called the 'National Careers Service'. I was booked onto a career consultation with a professional Careers Advisor to talk about my career paths and where I see myself in terms of the Career Ladder. During our career consultation, my Careers Advisor asked me, 'So what do you want to become when you grow older?'. And my response to that was vague and full of uncertainty. I did not think it through as my focus was on getting through my GCSE's and enjoying the long summer break ahead.

As a British Bangladeshi living in a Council Estate with members in the family on a low disposable income, there were familial pressures to be someone big and represent the Bangladeshi community and feel like a leader of the next generation of young people. There is still that notion of backward mentality amongst Asian families that the back home work ethic applies to how the Brits exercise hard work. Sadly, this has been the case for a while; however, the modern, technologically advanced economy we have now influences our way of thinking that an individual's career is determined through their personal discovery and challenges they face along the way. So, being told what I should become can strip away the freedom of being myself. I had thought to myself that this would be a personal journey for me that I would use this opportunity to discover what I really want to get into as a career. A career is never meant to feel so linear for the rest of your life. To me, it is a mathematical construction that allows you to 'trial and error' different career paths to establish a rewarding Career.

I responded to my Careers Advisor – 'I'm not quite sure what I want to become, but I'd like to become an IT Technician, or maybe work in a bank.'

So, my Career Advisor said, 'Okay, let's have a look at these roles and what qualifications and skills you require to undertake these roles'. She looked on the National Careers Service, and searched keywords for these roles and discussed what I needed to do to get there.

When I tell you the guidance, I received regarding exploring career paths was generic, it really was generic. I was still struggling to comprehend the 'ways' – strategies to ensure I met the goal – the 'ends. It is an abstract way of thinking, but what I am trying to get at is this – to get a successful CV that will help you land job interviews, you must go through the CV strategies which work to get to the end goal – a job interview.

To explore my career options further, I booked in an additional session with my Careers Advisor at Connexions in

Bow, East London. Connexions at the time was a centre you could go to if you require assistance from Career Advisors regarding CV writing, cover letter writing, and mock interview preparation. It was funded through a government initiative via the Tower Hamlets Council to drive employment opportunities for young people and improve their career prospects. I went to the session with the mindset that my Careers Advisor would support me in constructing my CV and polishing it up so it is 'job application ready' when applying for Retail and Admin roles. Again, the guidance around CV writing was basic as they asked me to list down the responsibilities and duties for each little work experience that I had from school and write a big paragraph for the 'Personal Profile' section. Logically, I felt that this was not adding value to my experience and did not see how this showcase to the employers that I have the relevant skills and calibre to be suitable for the roles I put myself forward for.

I was told to use the same CV for each role I applied for and not tailor it to the job specification.

Looking back now, the current guidance around CV writing by Career Coaches has improved, yet there is more to be done on how one tailor it personally to their skills and experiences. That is another important topic, but we will not delve into this for the purpose of this book.

And then in 2013, I began my university studies in Economics. At the time of applying to universities, I initially chose Business Management as the course subject due to studying Business in college. 18-year-old me in sixth form believed that studying a Business Management course would pave a path for me to become an entrepreneur one day. How wrong was I to realise that this wasn't the case! When I looked through the module handbooks in the first few weeks, I had to rethink my options as the course was boring me. So, I looked at doing a mathematical yet theoretical subject; so I chose Economics. Economics helped me understand the global economy, how the financial markets operate, and how trade of goods flows across countries by importing and exports between countries.

During my three years of university, I have been applying for hundreds of summer internships and part-time roles to gain a bit of pocket money to survive the economic climate and go about my days. There were many jobs and opportunities around; however, I still needed to cut it. The job market was quite competitive with a lot of students offering something different to make them more or less a suitable candidate for those roles. I can vaguely remember I was applying to the Big Four firms like Deloitte, PwC, KPMG, and constantly setting job alerts on Indeed and common job sites. I wasn't applying the strategies for applications and faced numerous rejections with the famous '***Unfortunately, we have decided not to shortlist you for an interview at this time. Do not let this deter you from applying for roles with us***' message. There were little to no resources that would have supported me with my applications.

Fast forward to Autumn 2016, I graduated from London Metropolitan University in Economics. I was able to find myself a Retail job during the Christmas Period. Finally, something! If it wasn't aligned with my degree, it did not matter as at that stage. I needed to acquire some experience to add to my CV and make it sparkle. So, I worked for a few weeks, then went onto working for other retail departments such as Next, WHSmith, Greggs, and One Stop Shop (Tesco's little partner you could say), and in schools as a SEN Teaching Assistant before applying consistently to the UK Civil Service.

Now that you have discovered my journey leading up to the Civil Service, I will highlight some of the key challenges I faced amidst the journey and how I overcame them, and what I'd do differently.

Personal Challenge #1

'As much as I wanted to secure a part-time role in my first year of university, it was an ongoing struggle to land one.'

What I did to OVERCOME this: Consistently applied and revised my strategies for applications.

What I would DO differently: Engage with the Careers & Employability Team in the University or alternatively find a mentor working in the industry to guide me in the right direction.

Personal Challenge #2

'Whilst studying at university, I would have hoped there would be informative and helpful presentations on application writing and LinkedIn. Unfortunately, there weren't any.'

What I did to OVERCOME this: Resorted to content online by checking on Recruitment Agency Sites for tips on application process, despite the information being generic and not as helpful.

What I would DO differently: Raise it with the Careers & Employability Team to push out tailored and relatable content to drive opportunities for students because paying a

£9,000 tuition fee a year to end up with no job after graduation isn't a joke. It's serious stuff.

Personal Challenge #3

*'When applying for entry level roles, I was asked for **x** amount of experience in **x, y and z** roles.'*

What I did to OVERCOME this: The little experience I had from doing some work experience in school as a Receptionist and Teacher's Postman and some experience working in the London Borough Office, I used all of it to sell myself to employers.

What I would DO differently: Gain more experience by putting myself forward for volunteering opportunities in the local area.

Personal Challenge #4

'When seeking support from others around how to stand out in Civil Service Applications, I was greeted with 'Have a look at the Civil Service Framework; it has everything you need.'

What I did to OVERCOME this: I spoke to my Work Coach at the Job Centre to review my work experiences and university studies. They helped me to see the impact I could create for the Civil Service Competencies.

What I would DO differently: Reach out to more industry professionals in the Civil Service on LinkedIn and create a first good impression by showing interest in Civil Service roles. Also, asking questions aligned to my work experiences and the roles would be good.

Key Takeaway Gems from this Chapter:

- You learn that challenges are not hurdles to your success. They support your growth, leading to that career, wherever you may land.
- Never belittle your work experiences and activities you took part in. In the grand scheme of things, they matter a lot. Definitely in the eyes of the Recruiter!
- If Rejection has taught me anything, it's that the role that is meant for me is on its way.

Chapter 2: Remedies to Imposter Syndrome at the Time of Applying

Imagine yourself as a student studying a course at university. You're amongst a crowd of other students who you don't know. Their backgrounds differ, their status and all that malarkey too. You look up to them and see that they're applying, just like you, getting job interviews and smashing it. The next day, you sit in the lecture theatre and hear a group of students manage to get into a Retail role. You've been doing the same thing like the rest, but it hasn't been working in your favour. You fear that you're not good enough to get into the roles due to your lack of experience. It's normal to feel imposter syndrome. Many of us have experienced it, and I want to bring your attention to some of the remedies which helped me overcome the imposter syndrome when I applied to the UK Civil Service.

Remedy #1:

Try your best not to focus on looking at others who secured roles. That will deter you from focusing on what you need to do to secure job interviews and job offers. It is about looking at your strengths and applying them to your applications. Also, you look at your weaknesses in the application process and turn them into strengths. Get more guidance from family, other students, friends, etc.

Remedy #2:

Have faith and belief in your skills and experience. If you analyse the skills you have, you'd be surprised how many you have acquired. Use them to your advantage on your applications. If you're still in doubt about your skills and experience, ask a Civil Service professional, and they will tell you and help you to believe in them as capabilities to do any role as long as they're applied in the right way and context.

Remedy #3:

What you may lack experience for can be something deemed as a continuous improvement (Kaizen) for you. For example, if you're considering applying for a Data Analyst role and one of the Essential Criteria points states that you need to be skilled in the use of Python and Power BI, they're two things you can self-learn through YouTube or study through books from your local library or bookshop. This approach will equip you with the necessary skills to apply not just for that role but other roles where there is a need for Data Analysis in organisations (in every case, there's a massive need for it. It's a high-income skill).

Remedy #4:

Competition fever can get in the way. What I mean by 'Competition Fever', you may ask me. It's a term I invented to imply that when you're looking through the Civil Service roles, you may be held back the fact that those currently working for the Civil Service will have more leverage and success in passing the sifting stage than someone applying externally. This is not always true. Coming from a graduate/retail background, I have mustered the confidence to build interpersonal skills that are transferable when applying for the Civil Service. I ensured the central focus was on '**ME**'. I thought about ways I could play with the words in my examples for the Civil Service Behaviours and really thought about how I could solidify my experiences to fit in well with the Success Profile Framework. This helped set me apart from those who were applying to the Civil Service with a higher calibre of skills and experience.

Remedy #5:

In the back of my mind, I have felt a lingering doubt that if I apply for Civil Service roles which have one vacancy that I won't have a chance to land a job interview and secure a job offer. With this, I shaped my way of thinking by telling myself that this is an open opportunity. An opportunity if not seized will limit every chance I have. What helped me the most with combating this lingering doubt my father telling me, 'If you don't give it a try, how will you ever see if it works in your favour or not.' And that hit me. I needed that constructive criticism to pull myself together and keep on going, no matter how anxious I felt at the time. And with a relentless and open mind, I applied for more Civil Service roles. I put in the quality and secured job interviews in the Department for Education, Department of Health and Social Care, Ministry of Defence, and other government departments.

Key Takeaway Gems from this Chapter:

- You learn that doubts will linger in your mind, but it's about reminding yourself that you have the potential to apply and be successful in the role you apply for. You just have to believe in yourself, forget the noise out there, and look at the things you do have. Self-belief and gratitude go hand in hand.
- You learn that competing with others who are doing way better than you is toxic for your Mental Health. So, you focus on how you can compete with yourself and become the very best like how Ash Ketchum from Pokemon selfishly thought about himself, and how he became a Pokemon Champion.
- Channel your Strengths and learn from them. That is when you will know that you're not an outlier; in fact, you're the authentic YOU!

Chapter 3: Civil Service Graded Structure

When I initially started my job search for a Civil Service role, I wasn't made aware of the Civil Service Grades and the structure for the roles. I applied for everything and anything and received rejections upon rejections because of the scattergun approach. I wouldn't recommend this approach at all. What I'd recommend is understanding how the Civil Service grades work in practice and check how your experiences and skills to date are aligned with the grades.

Below is my summary of the Civil Service Grades and what stage you need to be at to apply for roles in those grades:

Administrative Officer (AO) – This grade is entry-level so, you could apply for roles at this grade if you've left college or are studying in your first year at university. It is aimed at those who have some experience working in different roles ranging from 6 months to a year.

Executive Officer (EO) – This grade is junior level; so, you could apply for roles at this grade if you have experience in organising your workload, supporting a team, and demonstrating a basic level of management.

Higher Executive Officer (HEO) – This grade is middle management level. So, you could apply for roles at this grade if you graduated from university and have worked in a team coordination role, communicating with a range of stakeholders internally and externally. Or, have a junior level of management experience under your belt.

Senior Executive Officer (SEO) – This grade is middle, senior management level, so, you could apply for roles at this grade if you have a Master's degree, are trying to get promoted from an HEO role, or have a considerable amount of stakeholder engagement skills with senior officials to drive business activity.

Grade 7 (G7) – This grade is senior management level. So, you could apply for roles at this grade if you have experience in delivering through others and leading others in the right direction through business objectives. To obtain this role, you need to move around in HEO and SEO roles and master different areas of specialisation in the UK Civil Service, which will help accelerate your progression to G7.

Key Takeaway Gems from this Chapter:

- You learn that there are varying grades within the Civil Service from AO-G7 and above.
- As a Graduate who is looking to apply for the Civil Service, HEO is the Graduate Level for you to apply at.

- There are certain abilities you may need to unlock to apply for the set grades so you can make the most of the Civil Service Application Process.

Chapter 4:
Civil Service Application Process Cycles (Traditional Route Vs Fast Stream Route)

Wondering what the Civil Service Application Process is like if you are considering a Career in the Civil Service? Then this Chapter is for you, especially if you would like a brief understanding of which Route to take.

You could take one of two routes when applying for the Civil Service. One is the Traditional Route, which I took, where you apply on the Civil Service Jobs website and go through the process that way. And the other is the Fast Stream Route which is a graduate programme you could potentially apply for when you have graduated from a university (in any subject).

Below are application process cycles for both which I envision. Please note that this is subject to change, depending on the roles you apply for in the Civil Service. So, consider this as a general outline of how the application process can look like for both. This is how I envision from my experience of making applications through both routes.

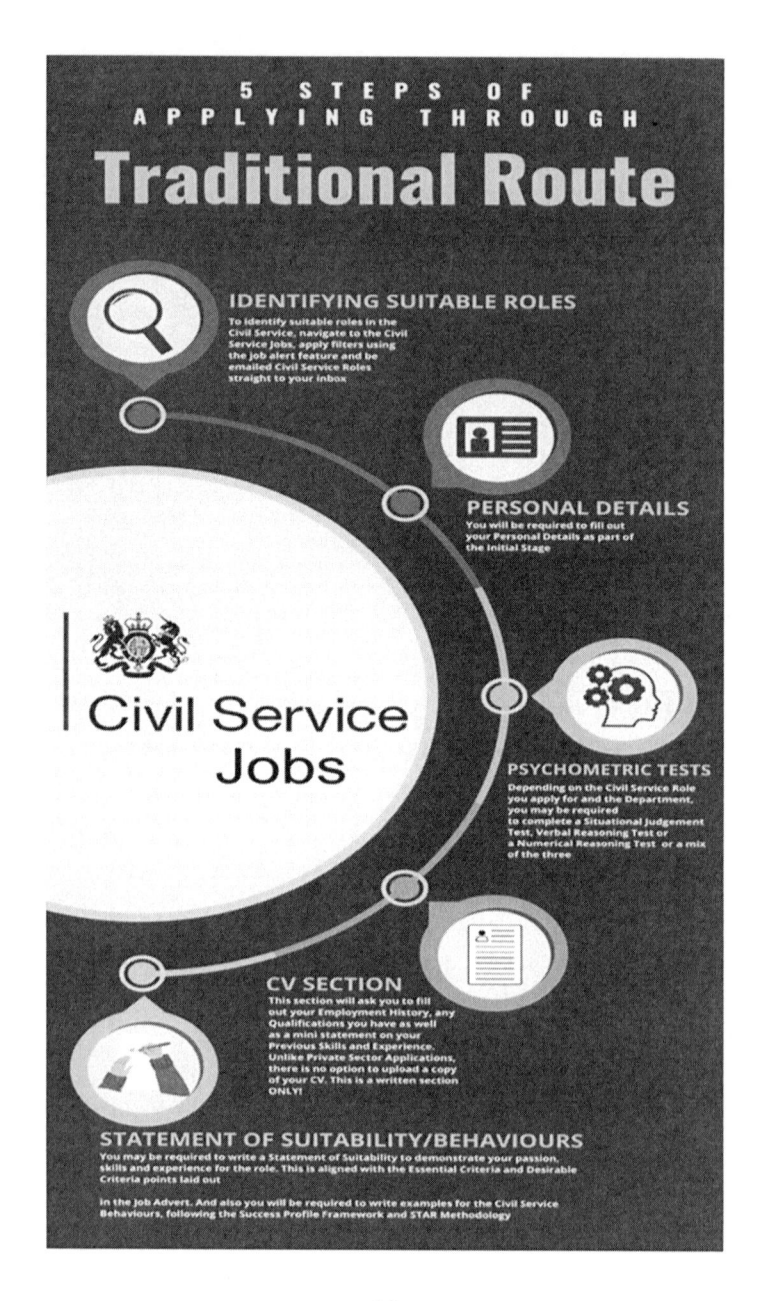

Traditional Route

5 STEPS OF APPLYING THROUGH Traditional Route

IDENTIFYING SUITABLE ROLES
To identify suitable roles in the Civil Service, navigate to the Civil Service Jobs, apply filters using the job alert feature and be emailed Civil Service Roles straight to your inbox

PERSONAL DETAILS
You will be required to fill out your Personal Details as part of the Initial Stage

Civil Service Jobs

PSYCHOMETRIC TESTS
Depending on the Civil Service Role you apply for and the Department, you may be required to complete a Situational Judgement Test, Verbal Reasoning Test or a Numerical Reasoning Test or a mix of the three

CV SECTION
This section will ask you to fill out your Employment History, any Qualifications you have as well as a mini statement on your Previous Skills and Experience. Unlike Private Sector Applications, there is no option to upload a copy of your CV. This is a written section ONLY!

STATEMENT OF SUITABILITY/BEHAVIOURS
You may be required to write a Statement of Suitability to demonstrate your passion, skills and experience for the role. This is aligned with the Essential Criteria and Desirable Criteria points laid out

In the Job Advert. And also you will be required to write examples for the Civil Service Behaviours, following the Success Profile Framework and STAR Methodology

Fast Stream Route

5 STEPS OF APPLYING THROUGH Fast Stream Route

REGISTERING YOUR INTEREST
To sign yourself up for the Civil Service Fast Stream, you can register your interest on the Civil Service Fast Stream Website where you will be alerted when the Application Cycle restarts again

PERSONAL DETAILS & CHOICES
There will be a section where you have to fill in your personal details and another section to select the schemes in order of priority. More info on the schemes can be found on the Civil Service Fast Stream Site

ONLINE TESTS
You will be required to complete a series of online tests ranging from your ways of working to Verbal Reasoning, Numerical Reasoning and Work Related Scenarios

PRE-RECORDED INTERVIEW
If successful in previous stages, you will be invited to record your responses to pre-recorded Interview Questions. This is to test your suitability for the Fast Stream Programme

ASSESSMENT CENTRE
Once you have completed all the other stages, you will have to attend an Assessment Centre where your skills and experience will be put to the test, demonstrating the Civil Service Values and Competencies

Civil Service Fast Stream

Key Takeaway Gems from this Chapter:

- There are two routes to applying to the UK Civil Service; Traditional and Fast Stream
- If you're looking to specialise in an area of work, the Fast Stream Route would be the one for you to take as it will be tailored to the career you're after.
- There is no inclination for you to go for the most common route. It solely depends on your interests and what you're really looking for in a career, but remember, there is an opportunity to explore different roles and progress internally within a department or across other government departments.

Chapter 5: Transferable Experiences Required for Civil Service Roles

In Chapter 3, we looked at the Civil Service Graded Structure, where we were able to understand which grade we can apply for roles at.

Now you may be wondering what type of experience you need to apply for Civil Service Roles.

Well…

For this, there really isn't a one-size-fits-all approach because there are many types of experience acceptable by the Civil Service unofficially, not officially, by the way.

I have invented a motto if you're in doubt whether your experiences are enough and that is:

"Any experience you currently have is valid when it comes to applying to the UK Civil Service."

To give you some context to how you may apply your experiences to Civil Service roles, I will share a story of my experiences before securing a Civil Service role.

As mentioned in the opening Chapter (1), I worked in Retail. Yes, Retail. What I found with Retail is it provides the foundation for Customer Service and felt basic as an example on an application for a Civil Service Role. I didn't see Retail in different angles until when I signed up to Benefits at the Job Centre Plus, my Work Coach was able to shed some light on my Retail experiences, despite not having a year or more of experience in retail. My Work Coach and I worked together in amending the retail and also Admin examples (from working for the Council Benefits Office). There was a framework that she recommended I use to structure my examples around. It was the Civil Service Framework (2018), now known as the **Success Profiles**.

For your reference, you can view the **Success Profiles Framework** by Googling "Success Profiles Behaviours", and it's the PDF version. Anyway, back to the story, she explained that the UK Civil Service uses the Framework to assess 9 behaviours during the application process and at the interview stage. Depending on the roles you apply, you're not assessed on all 9 of them. It's only up to a maximum of 6/7 behaviours. The common behaviours that tend to be assessed are **Seeing the Big Picture, Communicating & Influencing, Making Effective Decisions, Leadership, and Delivering at Pace**.

Then, my Work Coach asked me to send her my drafted behaviours for her to see if I'm using the correct technique (**STAR**) and good examples related to the behaviours. She pointed out that I was using a lot of jargon in my examples and not being concise in explaining the **Situation, Task, Actions, and Result**. Because I was new to writing the Civil Service Behaviours and had a bad habit of mentioning '**we**' and not '**I**' because in reality, and we did things together as a team. I have learned from my Work Coach to use basic English and not complicate it using technical language to throw the assessor off track.

For my experience working in Greggs, I was serving pastries during a busy lunch period. I had to prepare pastries and have them hot and ready for customers. I explained this example to my Work Coach who managed to get me thinking along the lines of the **Delivering at Pace** behaviour where the criteria stated that you have to mention the deadline you were working towards, how you met the deadline, and how you reassured customers whilst they were waiting longer than usual in the queue. As soon as I saw the bigger picture with my retail example, I was aback with my thoughts towards my Retail experience. My retail experience was not weak after all. It was strong. I just did not know how to word it in such a way that it is aligned with the Behaviours. Honestly, I did not know where to start, although I was pretty good at forming words and sentences for poems, but that's different to application writing, come on!

I was grateful towards my Work Coach for allowing me to see through my retail experiences and giving me the confidence to apply for AO and EO roles in the Civil Service.

I had a love-hate relationship with Retail, like having to put up with customers' frustration about me not packing their shopping bags fast enough. I'm not a robot with more than a human function to it. What I did love about working in retail is the team. They were supportive and willing to give you a hand when you were struggling with the tasks.

What did I learn in retail that assisted me in applying for Civil Service roles? Many things. Retail taught me how to communicate with a diverse range of customers on a daily basis and actually influence them to buy promotional products for a limited time only to boost revenue for the business. It's also allowed me to lead a team by sharing my knowledge on doing things a certain way and getting my team on board using my initiative in the workplace. Additionally, it's helped me to organise my time effectively when completing tasks such as restocking products on the shelves.

Another type of experience which I was able to transfer onto my job applications for the UK Civil Service, especially for AO and EO roles, I had my Admin work experience. My Sixth Form directed me to a work experience opportunity to work in the Mayor of Tower Hamlets Office (London Borough). I was like, okay, perfect, something I can actually put onto my CV and gain real experience in what it's like working in Admin. It was a two-week work experience opportunity. And blimey, when I started my first day in the office, I was welcomed in by an Asian fellow (People of Colour, representing my community). You do not see that often. He showed me around – the filing cabinets, folders, health and safety, etc. It was pretty relaxed. I wouldn't say I'd work there in the long run though as it was only to glamourise my CV with something different. I went through e-learning modules, updating Excel and organising an event for the Mayor of Tower Hamlets at the time. The admin skills were quite basic, if I say so myself. But what I took away from the admin experience was having the ability to streamline the process of organising information onto a computerised system from it starting off on paper. One other takeaway was the ability to interact with a range of stakeholders from different teams – people team, benefits team, and events management team. This is an essential skill to have when applying to the Civil Service as they will assess how you communicate with others and work collaboratively within a multidisciplinary team to achieve a shared goal.

Coming back to another retail experience. I did say I worked in a few retail places, however, this one was not the usual retail experience. I applied for some customer service roles on the Tesco Careers website. One day, I was in the library, don't ask me why. No, I did not go to the library to apply for jobs that day. I used the space to pick up a telephone interview call from a One Stop Shop Manager who asked me a series of questions to get to know me, my experience. He endeavoured to get back to me the next day to let me know I was successful, and that I'd been invited to a face-to-face interview in the store. I travelled from East London to South London for the interview. I was nervous and anxious because for me, it was the question of what if he asked why I did not stay in retail places for long, and why I was job hopping a lot? My answer was simple – learning about different types of retail and gathering a varied skill set to apply for better and bigger roles in the Civil Service. Obviously, I didn't mention 'Civil Service', otherwise, he'd think I do not want to be in retail in the long-run.

Besides the interview process, let me explain how the work was. When I tell you it was a very busy store, it really was. So many customers were queuing up at different times of the day or during certain days, yes 'busy days'. It was challenging as I was sorting out Hermes (currently known as Evri) deliveries as well as ensuring a fast and efficient service to the customers. This level of Retail experience was fast-paced and got me on my feet, thinking outside the box and going above and beyond for these customers. It felt exhausting – a repeat of the same task over and over again. The thing with retail right is that you're having to deal with challenging situations and use your independent thinking skills to work smarter but also faster. I wouldn't regret working for One Stop Shop because it helped me to work so much faster; for example, when I started as an Administrative Officer for the Civil Service, I was completing administrative tasks quickly to a very high standard. The feedback I reciprocated from my peers was 'how did you manage to get the work done so fast?', 'that was quick, you did what I asked and you delivered the work in a jiffy'.

Going forward, in Dec 2020, I started Careers Pal amidst a pandemic as well as the lack of resources and support for students whilst studying at university. The objective of Careers Pal is to help the underrepresented have a voice and be confident in applying for senior positions regardless of their background and lack of experience. I was able to take this initiative forward by signing up as an Academic Mentor to the Queen Mary University Flagship Mentoring Scheme called 'QMentoring'. I acquired transferable experiences of mentoring a first-year university student on CVs, cover letter writing, networking, and job interviews. Through this experience, I formed an example of my mentoring skills onto my applications for the Civil Service, especially aligning it to **Communicating and Influencing** Behaviour. The Success Profile Criteria states that you need to be able to use a range of different mediums of communication to help others understand a process of some sort and why the communication methods were effective in simplifying understanding for others.

Ever since I was a teenager, I knew I had a creative side to me. I used to do rapping, got into graphic design, singing, etc. So, to educate others on careers and point them in the right direction in their Career journey, I put myself forward and created a TikTok channel for Careers Pal and started recording myself in front of my phone camera, bearing in mind I was not comfortable talking to the camera. I was focusing on a lot of generic advice, but I constantly reflected on the delivery of my videos and tailored them to Civil Service. As soon as my videos were tailored to the Civil Service, I saw my TikTok going viral on the **FYP** (For You Page) and surpassing 50,000 views. What I learned from being a creative junkie is that it's a valuable skill to have in the Civil Service as there is that autonomy to test the waters by bringing your ideas forward in the workplace.

A final transferable experience that I felt was required to apply for Civil Service roles was Organising an Event. On LinkedIn, I used networking strategies to connect with other Civil Servants on the Civil Service Fast Stream as well as the Summer Internship Programmes, which the Civil Service provides each year. I was in a good position to organise an event, considering I studied an assignment in Sixth Form on how to run and manage a successful event. I designed the banner for the EventBrite page for students and graduates to sign-up for the event, bringing in my expertise in Graphic Design. I also promoted the event on my social media platforms to give students and graduates the opportunity to hear from Civil Servants their experiences working in top departments – HM Treasury, Ministry of Justice, and Department for Culture, Media & Sport (at the time – 2021). This was an informative session for students and graduates as they were exposed to the range of opportunities that Civil Service had to offer.

A surprising fact I want to share is that this experience was pivotal in driving my success in an interview for HM Treasury at the Executive Officer grade. I was asked what I was doing outside my Civil Service role that I enjoyed the most.

In summary, you could say every experience I endured working in Retail, Admin, Events, Marketing (Content Creation) was transferable and unique in their own ways which supported me in applying for Civil Service roles. And you can do the same by creating your own portfolio of experience. A good starting point would be to channel your strengths in your previous roles and pick out your best strength which you'd be happy to pursue further. It might be that very strength that will open the gate to Civil Service opportunities. Just remember Civil Service opportunities are endless, not limited. Any opportunity can knock on your door if you let it, and don't ever question your worth for not being good enough to apply.

Key Takeaway Gems from this Chapter:

- You learn that you do not need to have very professional work experience to apply for an entry-level in the Civil Service. Whatever experience you hold currently or have held previously matters. It is how you amplify your experience to align it with the role requirements that will get you through the process.
- In every experience you gather, you learn a thing or two, whether that's working in Retail as a Shop Floor

Assistant or working in an Office doing Administration Work, or sweeping the floors as a Cleaner. Use your experiences to your advantage by talking about the highs when going through a Civil Service Application.

Chapter 6:
Pros of Working For
The Civil Service

In this Chapter, I will be talking about how beneficial I found the Civil Service to be as well as providing commentaries from other Civil Servants of what their key pros have been so far, working in the Civil Service.

When starting in the Civil Service in 2018, I was exposed to endless opportunities to develop myself personally and professionally.

In my first 3 months of working in the Civil Service, one of the important mandates was to complete Mandatory Training as part of the Admin role I was doing.

Completing the mandatory training equips you with the knowledge and experience to take on the role responsibilities successfully.

Mandatory training was part of a probationary period. A probationary period is something Civil Service departments use to assess your performance in the role and help you achieve your goals in the Civil Service. It can be from 3-6 months depending on which Civil Service department you're working for.

I had set myself a target to complete the Mandatory Training in a matter of three weeks, as I was interested in getting into what it's like working in the Civil Service and carrying out my duties as a Civil Servant.

Having completed the Mandatory Training in a few weeks, I was able to inspire and motivate other Civil Servants in my team to complete their Mandatory Training. They were behind with their Mandatory Training as they experienced busy operational periods working in the Office at the time prior to Hybrid Working/Working from Home being the norm.

In the first month of working in the Civil Service, I was provided with a brief induction on the Health and Safety protocols as well as the Civil Service Values. The training was hands-on and required shadowing experienced colleagues. I was absorbing the information visually as I'm a visual learner. However, I was told I needed to make notes for my understanding and can refer to when I get stuck in terms of performing the Admin role to the best of my ability.

As 6 months flew by in my first posting in the Civil Service, I passed my probationary period with flying colours. I mastered every element of the administration role, which gave me the confidence to identify gaps in existing admin processes and look at ways of streamlining admin processes to support my immediate team and senior management team.

So, one of my key pros of working in an Admin role at the time was being able to bring in creative ingenuity by sharing my ideas with the team and implementing them to simplify the process of case transfers between Probation Offices across England and Wales. My ideas were listened to and valued, and they were able to rely on my IT skills to deliver a new initiative for the Probation Service.

Additionally, it was my Admin role that allowed me to capture key administrative processes through manual guides, as the materials I found on the processes were technical for new starters to understand. I prioritised the creation of guides for processes alongside admin duties by booking in some time to complete them and pause when there was urgent administrative work that required my attention. I ensured my Mental Health was not compromised when working extremely hard to put together the manuals for the administration team in the Probation Service.

By creating manuals for key administrative processes, I elevated my career in the Civil Service by being promoted to a management role and then subsequently securing a role in Business Analysis.

So, I believe the career progression is steady and progressive in the sense that you have immense support from your peers and your Line Manager. I made my Line Manager my career bestie, whom I was able to approach for ideas on which examples to use for the Civil Service Behaviours. They were willing to review my examples and help draft them for applications so I can put forward future applications for senior roles.

One final pro I wanted to highlight working for the Civil Service is they encourage professional development in terms of completing professional courses in the area you wish to specialise in or if it's applicable to the role you're doing. For example, I was able to undertake a project management course and complete an exam to gain the credentials for it. This course would have cost me a thousand pounds to complete in three days. So it is a privilege to be continuously learning new things and knowing that the Civil Service recognizes the importance of your learning and development and will provide funding for courses that will accelerate your career to extra heights in the foreseeable future.

Here are some commentaries from other Civil Servants on what they felt were key pros of working for the Civil Service:

Commentaries from other Civil Servants:

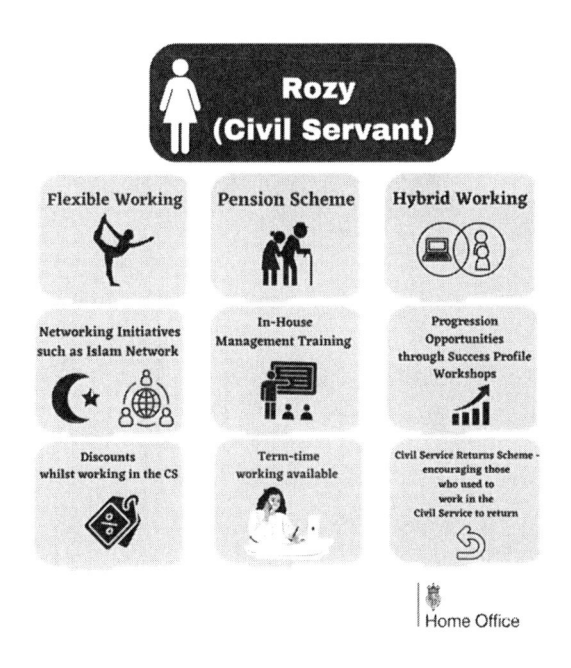

Rozy (Civil Servant)

- Flexible Working
- Pension Scheme
- Hybrid Working
- Networking Initiatives such as Islam Network
- In-House Management Training
- Progression Opportunities through Success Profile Workshops
- Discounts whilst working in the CS
- Term-time working available
- Civil Service Returns Scheme - encouraging those who used to work in the Civil Service to return

Home Office

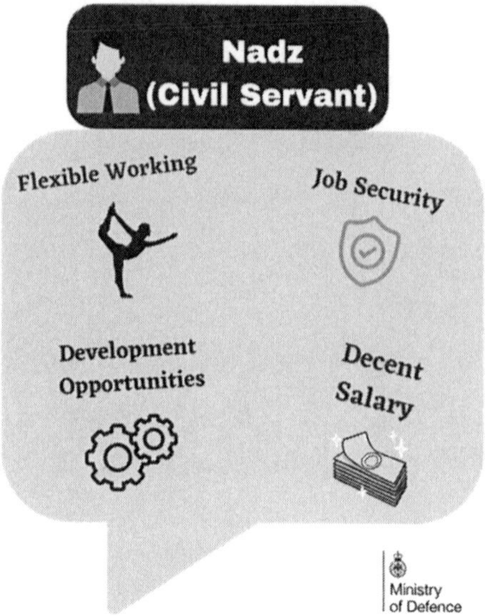

Nadz (Civil Servant)

- Flexible Working
- Job Security
- Development Opportunities
- Decent Salary

Ministry of Defence

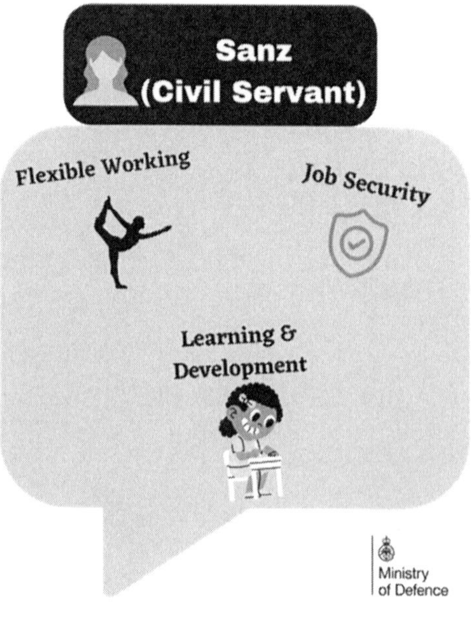

Sanz (Civil Servant)

- Flexible Working
- Job Security
- Learning & Development

Ministry of Defence

> **Jeme (Civil Servant)**
>
> Diverse Opportunities to work on your Self Development using Civil Service courses on the CSL Platform
>
> Career Progression Opportunities. CBF (Competency Based Framework) provides open communication with the line manager to discuss about your Career within the Organisation

Ministry of Justice

Key Takeaway Gems from this Chapter:

- My experience in the Civil Service has outlined personal and professional growth where I was able to build and develop new skills to support the wider team.
- There are endless opportunities working in the Civil Service – something for everyone, no matter your ethnicity, passion, disability, etc.
- Accredited Courses are funded by the Civil Service as long as you are doing the Civil Service Role in the relevant Profession.

Chapter 7:
Behaviours Structure & Analysis (AO-SEO Levels)

This Chapter will focus on one of the practical elements of the Civil Service Application process, which is writing examples for the Behaviours.

I will introduce you to a few different behavioural examples, starting from Administrative Officer all the way to the Senior Executive Officer grade.

You will understand the structure of the behaviours, what constitutes a good level example through a detailed analysis, and how they are scored using the Civil Service Scoring Criteria during the application sifting stage.

Deconstructing the Behaviours through Q's and Eureka Ideas

I'm not sure if you have read the Success Profile Behaviours PDF document, but I have. Personally I found it quite hard to understand what they are looking for in the 9 Behaviours, especially at the HEO/SEO grade. So here is a method I constructed to support your thought process when you're sourcing out examples to fit with the behaviours. By using this method, you will be able to apply chronological thinking when inventing your examples for the behaviours.

Seeing the Big Picture

- Does the work you carry out put a real focus on business needs? A business need is something that will have a positive impact in the workplace during busy, challenging periods. For example, if there are two administrators and the workload is such that it is not bearable for two administrators to take on, the business need would be ideally to recruit more administrators in the team to support the wider team function well.
- What are the values and aims of the company you work for? Now look at your work responsibilities, are they aligned with them? If so, how?
- How do you absorb the information of new issues surrounding your workplace and apply it in your workplace to show your understanding of them but also how you could develop other people's understanding of it, so it doesn't have a negative impact on how they perform in their roles?

Working Together

- In your current role, how do you establish professional relationships with your colleagues? Do you communicate effectively with them? Do you share your ideas with the team? Do you involve external colleagues outside your team in team meetings?
- How do you support others in the team?

- In meetings or in-person, do you listen to other's views, reflect, and show respect to them and not interrupt them when they're sharing their views?

Communicating & Influencing

- When communicating with others, do you take into account how they prefer to learn so you can tailor your communication using appropriate tone and language?
- How do you tend to communicate with others? Verbally, via written communication, or virtually? Or a mix of communication methods. Now, think about why your communication was beneficial to wider stakeholders and the business.
- Have you showcased something you've created to a colleague or a senior stakeholder to get their buy-in for a crucial project?

Making Effective Decisions

- At university, how did you make the right decisions when finding sources of information for a group presentation, research project, or module assignment? Did you look at the validity of the source, how reliable it is, and how authentic it is to be added to your work?
- Did you use a step-by-step approach when making decisions? If so, how effective was the approach when arriving at your decisions?

- Before you made your decisions, have you had a thought about how they would have an impact on other stakeholders and the business? In particular, would there be any setbacks if you implement these decisions?

Delivering at Pace

- Was there a target deadline for a piece of the project you were working on? If so, how did you use your organisational skills to prioritise important work alongside other important work priorities?
- When working towards a tight deadline, do you consider '**quality**' over quantity for your work? If so, how do you maintain quality in your work?
- What tools do you use to organise your work and ensure it meets the deadline early? Do you use Microsoft Planner, MS Outlook Reminders, or To-Do Lists?

Managing a Quality Service

- There are targets that your manager may have set for you to hit. How do you ensure you meet those targets in your place of work whilst considering customer's needs as well as business needs?
- What is one thing you have done that required you to go above and beyond for others in the team? Now, think about how that resulted in success for the organisation in the long run.

- What strategies have you used to resolve a challenge the business was facing? How did you use those strategies to help the business prosper?

Leadership

- In your place of work, have you seized the opportunity to train new joiners in the team? If so, how did you lead them in the right direction to help meet business objectives and retain staff?
- Did you use your initiative in bringing people together through engaging activities? How did you enable an inclusive working practice through these activities and boost their morale in the workplace?
- Were you able to inform your colleagues regarding different networks they can join to become involved in what is going on in the organisation? How did you get them on board with a diverse range of networks?

Developing Self and Others

- Every role you have experienced so far, you have completed e-learning modules for the role. How did you pass on the knowledge from e-learning to your role as a way of developing yourself?
- Experienced in your current role? Then why not share your expertise with others in your team so they can develop themselves, acquire new skills, and progress upward in their career.

- Has your workplace offered additional training to help you and others upskill in your role? Yes? Use this to your advantage and build up your portfolio of expertise. You will need it wherever you go, especially when pivoting your career.

Changing and Improving

- Find out what needs to be fixed at your workplace and look for a solution to it. What is one issue you identified and did something about to improve the workplace? For example, when I was working as an Administrator, the issue I identified was that most of the information was put on paper, and so I wanted to change that. I suggested the idea of having the information on a spreadsheet where it can be accessible and edited easily without causing a headache for everyone in the team. This ensured a streamlined approach and accelerated how work was being completed
- Were you able to get buy-ins from senior stakeholders when putting forward suggestions for change? How did you present your suggestions to them? PowerPoint, in-person, email, etc.
- How did you keep others up to date with the changes from start to finish and gather input from team members regarding what type of improvements they wanted to see?

Cross-Referencing Exercise

To help make it easier for you to write high-scoring examples, I have come up with an exercise that we will go through to demonstrate how a Behavioural example is written. I call this exercise the *'Cross-Referencing Exercise.'*

For the purpose of this exercise, I will be using one of my examples for **Communicating and Influencing** behaviour which I scored a **6** in the application sifting stage.

Exercise Part 1: Gathering Your Thoughts

Right this moment, I want you to put the Success Profile Framework aside. We will come back to it later.

For now, I would like you to get a piece of paper, draw a circle in the middle of it, and write '**Communicating and Influencing**' inside the circle.

Once you have done that, I would like you to draw four lines going outwards. These lines will be used to form your thoughts.

With the first line you've drawn on the left side of your paper, draw a circle with '**Communication**' inside it. And with the third line you've drawn on the right-hand side of your paper, draw a circle with '**Influence**' inside it.

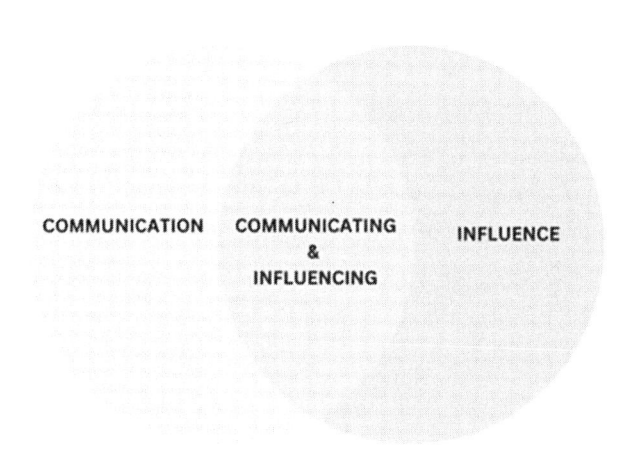

| COMMUNICATION | COMMUNICATING & INFLUENCING | INFLUENCE |

Now that we have the right elements in place, we can start gathering thoughts about what Communicating and Influencing look like.

For the '**Communication**' circle, draw 3-4 lines coming out of it. Now think of ways you communicated either at university, through volunteering, or at work (in particular, I would like you to write down methods of communication you used.

What I have come up with in terms of ways I communicated was in the context of a university. One way of communication was via verbal communication through my audience (students and the lecturer). The method I used was via a PowerPoint presentation on international migration. Another way of communication was written communication with my lecturer. The method I used was writing an informative and detailed essay on the challenges people faced in migrating to the UK for better standards of living.

Let's move on to the '**Influence**' circle you've drawn. Like the '**Communication**' circle, I would like you to draw 3-4 lines coming out of it. And then I want you to go back to the communication methods you've written and ask yourself: who can I influence and get a buy-in from using my ways of communication? To rephrase it simply, what influence do I have on others through my communication methods?

What I've come up with in terms of ways of influencing was in the context of Leadership. For example, when working as an Admin Manager for the Probation Service, I observed and identified a lack of structure in terms of induction for new Case Administrators joining the Civil Service for the first time. I used my initiative to lead a new joiner's training project where I would prepare a training pack and a training checklist for Case Administrators coming from a non-civil service background. I presented my idea to the Head of Probation Delivery and the Business Manager for their consent, I explained the benefit of having a structure for the Case Administrator's induction, which was to help support new starters to learn at their own pace and develop their knowledge in a new area of work. This influenced the Senior Officials to be open to a new approach to the new joiner's induction plan, which would help deliver an outstanding service in the Probation environment.

Exercise Part 2: Find your Reasoning

In the previous exercise, we looked at how to get ourselves thinking about a range of communication methods and how they are used to influence a person or people in the team.

What we will look at now is Reasoning. I would like you to go back to your communication methods you used in the previous exercise and have a think through the '**WHY?**'.

It is a question of why you have chosen your Communication Strategy. Finding your Why will help you to find the purpose of using the Communication Strategy as a means to influence someone or a team. To help you, I have an example that will put this into perspective. So, when I was a Case Administrator for the Probation Service, I identified that there was no structure in training new joiners regarding key administrative processes. So, when I was informed that there would be a few new administrators joining the admin team, I first understood their learning styles. They were visual learners who liked to try doing the work themselves and learning from it. This prompted me to construct and deliver scenario-based exercises on drafting letters. My reasoning behind this Communication Strategy was to help introduce the work Case Administrators do and ease them into understanding one of the Administrative Processes, mastering it, and moving onto the next Administrative Process. Through this way, they were able to engage effectively in the work and use it as a learning curve in their journey as a Case Administrator.

What we have learnt from my choice of Communication Strategy is the importance of identifying the learning needs of a diverse range of people and tailoring your communication style to meet their needs, so they can demonstrate their willingness and enthusiasm to learn on the job.

Exercise Part 3: Making the Link to the Success Profile Framework

Let's now look at how to make your example link to the Success Profile Framework.

The easiest way to ensure the example you're writing hits the points from the Civil Service Success Profile is by simply referring to it. You can go back and forth with it as much as you want, so you're not going off-topic.

We can easily find ourselves talking about other behaviours in a behavioural example which focuses on one behaviour. That's common because some behaviours overlap and tend to be similar in their own rights; for example, Working Together behaviour does require an element of communication and vice versa. Let's not fall into that trap.

For this exercise, I would like you to open up the Success Profile Behaviours PDF file. It would be easier to do this on your computer or laptop so you can copy and paste easily. Now, what I would like you to do is find the behaviour you're working on and at the grade level you're applying for (AO, EO, HEO, SEO, etc.).

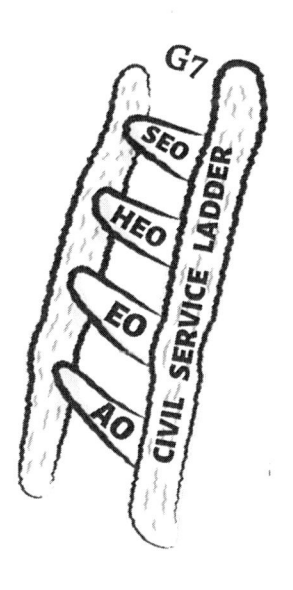

Once you have found the Behaviour, open up the Notes App, copy, and paste the criteria for that Behaviour into it.

Onto the fun part, which is drafting the example and making the link to the Success Profile Framework. To start drafting your example and making this link, highlight the key words from the criteria for the Behaviour. In this example, we will be looking at the EO grade level for Communicating and Influencing. The keywords derived from this criterion are ***communicate, orally, writing, communication channel, interact, listen, and value.***

When writing your example for communicating and influencing at the EO grade level, think about the following questions to keep a coherent structure to your example:

1. ***How did you communicate messages orally and in writing? For e.g., face-to-face communication (oral) and email correspondence/letters (writing).***
2. ***What communication channel did you consider?***
3. ***What was your method of interaction with other stakeholders in the team?***
4. ***How did you ensure you were actively listening to others in the team and being open to their perspectives on things?***

By undertaking this exercise, you will have mastered how to structure your experiences in a way that meets the Success Profile Criteria.

Scoring Criteria for Behaviours

Before we move onto analysing examples from AO-SEO levels, I would like to draw your attention to the Scoring Criteria, which is used as part of the Recruitment Process when sifting through the Behaviours.

Below, you will find the Scoring Criteria for Behaviours. The benchmark score to get shortlisted for an interview is a **4**, but this score can be raised if there is a large number of applications for the role you applied for. You will be notified of this if they do this.

Behaviours are assessed using the following scoring criteria:

1 – No demonstration
2 – Very little demonstration

3 – Moderate level of demonstration
4 – Acceptable level of demonstration – Benchmark Score to pass the Application Sift
5 – Good level of demonstration
6 – Strong demonstration
7 – Excellent demonstration

Connecting Retail Examples with Behaviours (Administrative Officer Level)

To help you angle Retail examples with Behaviours at AO Level, I will be using a dummy example to illustrate a good example with an analysis of that behaviour and a bonus tip to get extra marks.

Retail Example – Delivering at Pace

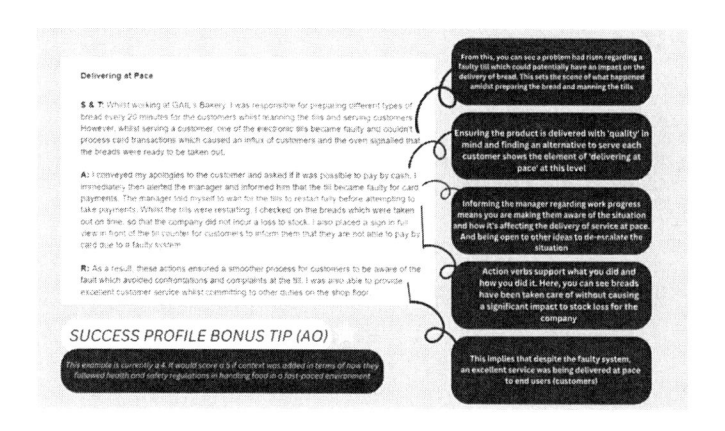

Delivering at Pace

S & T: Whilst working at GAIL's Bakery, I was responsible for preparing different types of bread every 20 minutes for the customers whilst manning the tills and serving customers. However, whilst serving a customer, one of the electronic tills became faulty and couldn't process card transactions which caused an influx of customers and the oven signalled that the breads were ready to be taken out.

A: I conveyed my apologies to the customer and asked if it was possible to pay by cash. I immediately then alerted the manager and informed him that the till became faulty for card payments. The manager told myself to wait for the tills to restart fully before attempting to take payments. Whilst the tills were restarting, I checked on the breads which were taken out on time, so that the company did not incur a loss to stock. I also placed a sign in full view in front of the till counter for customers to inform them that they are not able to pay by card due to a faulty system.

R: As a result, these actions ensured a smoother process for customers to be aware of the fault which avoided confrontations and complaints at the till. I was also able to provide excellent customer service whilst committing to other duties on the shop floor.

From this, you can see a problem had risen regarding a faulty till which could potentially have an impact on the delivery of bread. This sets the scene of what happened amidst preparing the bread and manning the tills

Ensuring the product is delivered with 'quality' in mind and finding an alternative to serve each customer shows the element of 'delivering at pace' at this level

Informing the manager regarding work progress means you are making them aware of the situation and how it's affecting the delivery of service at pace. And being open to other ideas to de-escalate the situation

Action verbs support what you did and how you did it. Here, you can see breads have been taken care of without causing a significant impact to stock loss for the company

This implies that despite the faulty system, an excellent service was being delivered at pace to end users (customers)

SUCCESS PROFILE BONUS TIP (AO)
This example is currently a 4. It would score a 5 if context was added in terms of how they followed health and safety regulations in handling food in a fast-paced environment

Connecting Admin Examples with Behaviours (Executive Officer Level)

To help you angle Admin examples with Behaviours at EO Level, I will be using a dummy example to illustrate a good example with an analysis of that behaviour and a bonus tip to get extra marks.

Admin Example – Changing and Improving

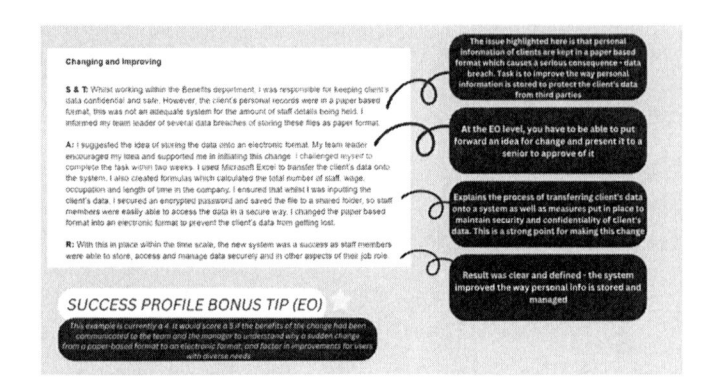

Changing and Improving

S & T: Whilst working within the Benefits department, I was responsible for keeping client's data confidential and safe. However, the client's personal records were in a paper based format, this was not an adequate system for the amount of staff details being held. I informed my team leader of several data breaches of storing these files as paper format.

A: I suggested the idea of storing the data onto an electronic format. My team leader encouraged my idea and supported me in initiating this change. I challenged myself to complete the task within two weeks. I used Microsoft Excel to transfer the client's data onto the system. I also created formulas which calculated the total number of staff, wage, occupation and length of time in the company. I ensured that whilst I was inputting the client's data, I secured an encrypted password and saved the file to a shared folder, so staff members were easily able to access the data in a secure way. I changed the paper based format into an electronic format to prevent the client's data from getting lost.

R: With this in place within the time scale, the new system was a success as staff members were able to store, access and manage data securely and in other aspects of their job role.

- The issue highlighted here is that personal information of clients are kept in a paper based format which causes a serious consequence - data breach. Task is to improve the way personal information is stored to protect the client's data from third parties
- At the EO level, you have to be able to put forward an idea for change and present it to a senior to approve of it
- Explains the process of transferring client's data onto a system as well as measures put in place to maintain security and confidentiality of client's data. This is a strong point for making this change
- Result was clear and defined - the system improved the way personal info is stored and managed

SUCCESS PROFILE BONUS TIP (EO)
This example is currently a 4. It would score a 5 if the benefits of the change had been communicated to the team and the manager to understand why a sudden change from a paper-based format to an electronic format; and factor in improvements for users with diverse needs

Connecting Content Creation and Mentoring Examples with Behaviours (Higher Executive Officer Level)

To help you angle Content Creation and Mentoring examples with Behaviours at HEO Level, I will be using two dummy examples to illustrate good examples with an analysis of the behaviours and bonus tips to get extra marks.

Mentoring Example – Managing a Quality Service

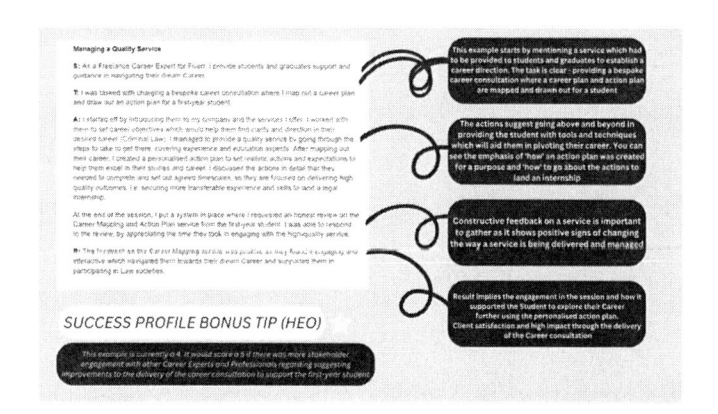

Content Creation Example – Delivering at Pace

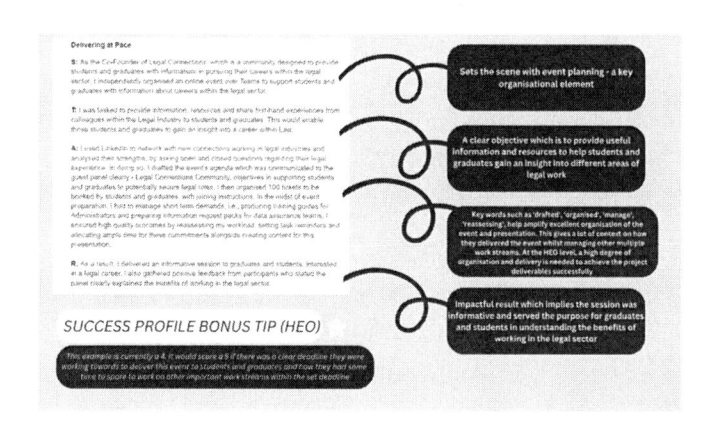

Connecting Analytical Examples with Behaviours (Senior Executive Officer Level)

To help you angle Analytical examples with Behaviours at the SEO Level, I will be using a dummy example to illustrate a good example with an analysis of that behaviour and a bonus tip to get extra marks.

Analytical Example – Seeing the Big Picture

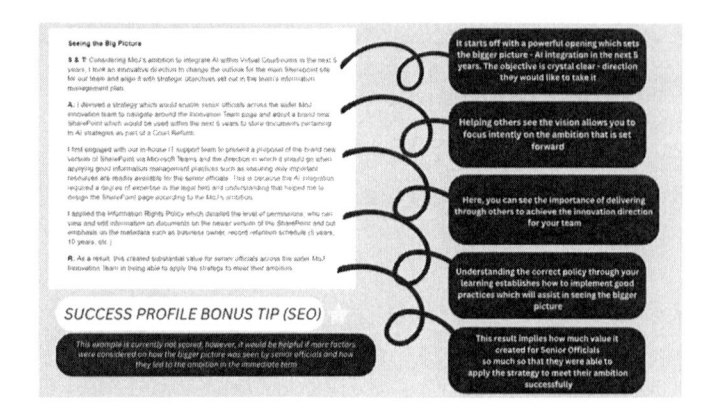

Seeing the Big Picture

S & T: Considering MoJ's ambition to integrate AI within Court-rooms in the next 5 years, I took an innovative direction to change the outlook for the main SharePoint site for our team and angle it with strategic objectives yet out in the team's information management plan.

A. I derived a strategy which would enable senior officials across the wider MoJ innovation team to navigate around the Innovation Team page and adopt a brand new SharePoint which would be used within the next 5 years to store documents pertaining to AI strategies as part of a Court Reform.

I first engaged with our in-house IT support team to present a proposal of the brand new version of SharePoint via Microsoft Teams and the direction in which it should go when applying good information management practices such as ensuring only important resources are readily available for the senior officials. This is because the AI integration required a degree of expertise in the legal field and understanding that helped me to design the SharePoint page according to the MoJ's ambition.

I applied the Information Rights Policy which detailed the level of permissions, who can view and edit information on documents on the newer version of the SharePoint and put emphasis on the metadata such as business owner, record retention schedule (5 years, 10 years, etc.).

R: As a result, this created substantial value for senior officials across the wider MoJ Innovation Team in being able to apply the strategy to meet their ambition.

SUCCESS PROFILE BONUS TIP (SEO)
This example is currently not scored, however, it would be helpful if more factors were considered on how the bigger picture was seen by senior officials and how they led to the ambition in the immediate term.

- It starts off with a powerful opening which sets the bigger picture - AI integration in the next 5 years. The objective is crystal clear - direction they would like to take it
- Helping others see the vision allows you to focus intently on the ambition that is set forward
- Here, you can see the importance of delivering through others to achieve the innovation direction for your team
- Understanding the correct policy through your learning establishes how to implement good practices which will assist in seeing the bigger picture
- This result implies how much value it created for Senior Officials so much so that they were able to apply the strategy to meet their ambition successfully

Key Takeaway Gems from this Chapter:

- There is a way to draft and write examples for the Civil Service Behaviours as depicted from the dummy examples we used – **examples need to be concise, clear, in detail and reflect on the 'how' in actions**
- Civil Service Behaviours are scored from **1-7, 7** being outstanding demonstration and **1** resulting to no demonstration.

- Deconstructing Behaviours allows you to understand clearly what each Behaviour is looking for. It breaks down the Success Profile Framework into bite-size chunks to aid your learning and application of effective examples for Civil Service Roles.

Chapter 8:
Personal Statement Structure & Analysis (EO-SEO Levels)

As well as having to write Behaviours for a Civil Service Application, you also are required to demonstrate your suitability for the role you've placed great interest and passion in. This is called a Suitability Statement, also known as a Personal Statement.

In this Chapter, we will unravel the types of Personal Statement you will be asked to write for the roles you apply for within the Civil Service.

It will then tackle the misconceptions of Civil Service Personal Statement Writing as there is a contrasting distinction between it and that of a Suitability Statement for a Private Sector Job Application.

Lastly, we will explore sample Personal Statements and provide a breakdown of what is good about them and how they are scored using the Personal Statement Scoring Criteria (**1-7**).

Types of Civil Service Personal Statement

This section of the Chapter will explain the many types of Personal Statement which have their set of requirements which need to be met.

Skills and Experience-Based Personal Statement

For the majority of the Civil Service Roles, you will come across, you will be asked to demonstrate how you meet the Essential and Desirable Criteria Points through the skills and experience you developed in your current and previous roles. This is to help them assess the **Ability** element of the **Success Profile Framework** where they can understand if you have the relevant or transferable skill set to take on the Civil Service Role you're about to apply for.

Behaviours Based Personal Statement

Sometimes, when reviewing the job specification for Civil Service Roles, you may possibly be asked to write a Personal Statement which **ONLY** requires examples following the **STAR** format to demonstrate the Behaviours needed to be competent for the Civil Service Role you're going for. So, this requires a level of meeting the points from the **Success Profile Framework** at the Civil Service Grade you're going for.

Misconceptions of Personal Statement Writing

There are some mishaps or misconceptions when it comes to writing a Personal Statement for a Civil Service Application.

One of the main misconceptions of Personal Statement Writing is that some individuals have felt the need to apply the skills of writing a Private Sector Cover Letter in the context of a Civil Service Personal Statement. This is wrong in two of many ways; firstly, with a Cover Letter, the format is such that it begins with an introduction to why you're applying for a role and how you have come across it, as well as briefly touching on your passion for the role and what you can bring to the team.

In contrast, a Civil Service Personal Statement starts with an opening which has a hook to grab the attention of the assessor. To do this, you will need to conduct empirical research and speak to Civil Service Professionals for greater insight into the areas being focused on for the role. The assessor reading the Personal Statement would want to follow through with it to identify the impact and achievements within your role and experiences.

Secondly, applying the Private Sector Cover Letter Strategy to a Civil Service Personal Statement means that you will find yourself using a lot of jargon, and the tone of language used would be vague and brief. Because of this, you will fail to hit the mark required for you to be shortlisted for an Interview.

A Civil Service Personal Statement is structured in a way that follows a concise and coherent format – enabling the use of simple English communicated in layman terms. We will explore this in greater detail in the Personal Statement Analysis section to show you how one is drafted and written to score top marks, which will help you land a Civil Service Job Interview.

Personal Statement Scoring Criteria

1. No positive evidence of Essential Criteria

2. Limited positive evidence of Essential Criteria
3. Moderate level of demonstration of Essential Criteria
4. Acceptable demonstration of Essential Criteria was demonstrated – Benchmark score to be shortlisted for an Interview
5. Good demonstration of Essential Criteria – Substantial positive evidence
6. Strong demonstration including some evidence of going above and beyond at this level
7. Outstanding demonstration – Strong evidence of going above and beyond at this level

Word Count for Personal Statement

The Personal Statement for a Civil Service Application can vary in terms of how many words you are required to write. The word limit can be as minimum as 250 words to a maximum word limit being 1250 words. This depends on how simple or complex the essential and desirable criteria points are.

250 words – This word count may be short, which can make you question how on earth, you will be able to demonstrate your skills and experience for a Civil Service Role. Simple – you have to look back at your previous experiences and skills and assess how strongly they meet the Essential Criteria points. There is no introduction needed for a very short Personal Statement; however, it would be helpful to amplify your skills and experience and create the strongest link to the Person Specification. Think about how you would write a compelling start and end to a short statement to engage the assessor at the time of sifting for consideration to the next stage – Interview.

500 words – This word count will amount to no more than a page of how strongly you demonstrate your skills and experience to meet the Essential Criteria and some Desirable Criteria points.

750 words – This word count will amount to a page and a half of how strongly you demonstrate your skills and experience to meet the Essential Criteria and some Desirable Criteria points.

1000 words – This word count will amount to two pages and a bit of how strongly you demonstrate your skills and experience to meet the Essential Criteria and some Desirable Criteria points.

1250 words – This word count will amount to two pages and a little more flipping onto the next page of how strongly you demonstrate your skills and experience to meet the Essential Criteria and some Desirable Criteria points.

Personal Statement Analysis

This is where it gets practical. We will now go through a few samples Civil Service Personal Statements from varying grades (**EO-SEO**) and analyse them through a simple breakdown analysis to help you understand where marks are being allocated for which parts are cut for shortlisting. But before we do, there is a Personal Statement Writing Strategy

Exercise I invented to help you draft your very own one. This will be good practice, especially when you have no clue how to gather your thoughts and think of a structure for a Civil Service Personal Statement.

Personal Statement Writing Strategy Exercise

Part 1 of 3 – Line up your experiences, skills and personal achievements

For Part 1 of this exercise, I would like you to jot down on a piece of paper or a Microsoft Word Document your relevant experiences and skills. You could prefer to do this in a bullet-pointed style – however, you would like to do this which is purely your choice. Now line them up in order of simplicity and complexity of work, as this will help gauge how easy or difficult it was for you to build and develop them throughout each job role. We will come back to this element in Part 3 of this Exercise.

Part 2 of 3 – Understand the Essential Criteria and Desirable Criteria points

This Part of the Exercise will require a basic level of understanding of the Essential Criteria and Desirable Criteria points. What I would like you to do is to have a look at a Civil Service Role you're interested in on the Civil Service Jobs Site, scroll through the job specification and look for the Criteria section. You'll find that what is common across the Essential Criteria points is you have to have excellent communication skills. If we break this down in simple terms, it means that you need to be able to demonstrate strong communication skills using effective communication methods. We can communicate important information to a diverse range of audience.

Now going through the Criteria section, what can you highlight from the points? Do they have relevance to the role? How important are the points for you to demonstrate them through your experiences, skills and personal achievements? These questions are to be asked as a reflection and understanding to aid you in bringing relevant expertise to the role you're applying for, which moves onto the final part of the exercise – linking your experiences, skills and personal achievements with the Criteria.

Part 3 of 3 – Link your experiences, skills and personal achievements with the Criteria

The finale! This final Part of the Exercise will assist you in linking your experiences, skills and personal achievements with the Criteria. I hope you will remember in the first part of the Exercise; I asked you to prepare relevant skills, experiences and personal achievements and line them up. Now, the final step is for you to open up a blank Word document, highlight all the Essential Criteria and Desirable Criteria points, right-click COPY, then right-click PASTE onto the blank Word document. Then, space them out and add Role, Brief Example of the Skill/Experience and the Impact. Voila, you have a structure in place and can form the base layer for your Civil Service Personal Statement.

Breakdown Analysis of Personal Statements (EO-SEO)

For this segment of the Personal Statement Chapter, we will explore a breakdown of sample Personal Statements ranging from EO-SEO grades using a template style format. This will aid your understanding of the structure, with the hope of helping you structure your very first Civil Service Personal Statement.

Personal Statement for an Internal Role (EO) – Expression of Interest (EOI) (500 words)

Sample Personal Statement Template (EO - 500 words)

I am writing to apply for the [specified role you're applying for] within [state department you're applying for]. I am keen on applying [state what skills and experience you intend to bring to the organisation]

[In this paragraph, you can talk about the skills and experience you have gained, providing different scenarios and how they are linked to the Essential Criteria]

[For this paragraph, you can elaborate further with different skills and experience and emphasising on the 'how' a bit more. Bonus points if you can make a clear link to the Essential Criteria by backing up your examples with substantial evidence]

[An additional paragraph to demonstrate how your skills and experience have developed to give you the ability to carry out the responsibilities specified in the person specification]

[A brief paragraph to demonstrate other transferable skills and experience to make you suitable for the role]

[Concluding paragraph to reiterate your passion for the role and how you acquire the skill set to undertake the role you're applying for]

Personal Statement for an Across Government Approach Role (HEO) (Internal) (250 words)

Sample Personal Statement Template (HEO - 250 words)

As [specify current role and organisation you work for], I am responsible for [state what you were responsible for and why]. Recently, I have been applying my [add the skills you have been developing] from having studied [insert subject areas] where I analysed [specify multiple sources and how info was conveyed]. This aligns well with the role, [specify which role you're applying for] as it allows me to [make the link to the Essential Criteria point] [then make another link to the Essential Criteria point and back it up with evidence from previous experiences]. Furthermore, having led colleagues in the [specify department], whilst covering a colleague, [emphasise on other Essential Criteria Points with valid examples from previous experiences]. [describe the approach you used to ensure consistency in processes and outstanding levels of customer service - subject to the Essential Criteria for the role as this can vary role to role]

Personal Statement for an External Approach Role (SEO) (External Vacancy) (750 words)

Sample Personal Statement Template (SEO - 750 words)

My [specify skills you built in your current role] helped me secure a promotion to a [specify role you moved onto], where I was responsible for [state what you were responsible for and why]. I applied my [specify the skills relevant to the Essential Criteria - either built from university, work or elsewhere] where I analysed [mention varied sources and how they were conveyed]. This translates into the role of a [specify which role you're applying for] as it honed my [make mention of the Essential Criteria Point and back it up with evidence from previous experiences] [more emphasis on another Essential Criteria Point with another example from previous/current experiences]. Moreover, having led [specify team/s you managed and from which department] [talk about how you communicated and the approach you took in the end]

As a [role] for the [department/organisation], I was involved with stakeholder engagement through [specify stakeholder activities you coordinated]. Stakeholders involved [list out the different stakeholders concerned]. I engaged with them to ensure [specify objectives you had to achieve]. This objective was achieved by [how was this objective achieved?]. [mention other tasks you completed and established an effective stakeholder network].

In addition, when engaging in [mention type of meetings you were involved in], I [specify how you engaged in meetings through tailored communication methods]. [give examples of different scenarios of senior engagement and project delivery - subject to Essential Criteria as it varies role to role]. It required approvals from [specify the people who had to sign this off] before releasing the implementation/strategy. The outcome of this was that [mention what this meant for the wider team and how significant it was to have the documentation]

[use ending phrases such as 'in finality', 'overall', 'lastly'], my previous roles allowed me to [mention what you learned from your previous role. What skills did you take away from working at your previous workplace]. [mention other elements of your skills and experience to fit well with the Criteria Points where necessary]

Key Takeaway Gems from this Chapter:

- It is **IMPORTANT** to note that the layout for a Personal Statement when applying for Civil Service Jobs is different to a Statement for a Private Sector Application.
- There are two types of Civil Service Personal Statement: **Skills-Based Statement** focusing on Essential and Desirable Criteria Points and **Behaviours Based Statement** focusing on the demonstration of Civil Service Behaviours.
- Maximum Word Limit for a Civil Service Personal Statement varies from **250 words – 1250 words**. This is dependent on what the Civil Service Department has set for their job posting as well as the Civil Service Role you apply for.

Chapter 9:
Ace Any Civil Service Interview (Face-To-Face, Pre-Recorded, Virtual)

In the previous chapters, we discovered how the Civil Service Application Process works through writing Behaviours to how you can write a scoring Personal Statement.

And so, it comes to the finale – yes, the Interview stage if you're successful at the sifting stage.

Interviews can be daunting if you make them out to be; however, I have got some tricks and tips under my sleeve to help prepare you for them and make you feel confident in your approach.

Before we delve into this chapter, let's have a look at the format of Civil Service Interviews to give you a better understanding of what to expect.

Types of Civil Service Interviews

When you receive an email notification on your phone to say you have been selected for a job interview, that is when you will know there will be another email to follow regarding the type of civil service interview you will be undertaking.

In the Civil Service, you will come across three types of interviews: face-to-face, virtual, and pre-recorded.

Face-to-Face Interviews

Face-to-Face Interviews are done in a more formal setting in an office environment where you get to communicate face-to-face with the interview panel members in a meeting room.

This type of Civil Service Interview requires you to stay organised by getting the essential documents such as your Right to Work (RTW) for identification and verification purposes.

Don't forget that you can take your notes to a face-to-face interview as long as it's bullet-pointed and straight to the point. Scripts are not allowed as they are looking to see if you can bring your personality into the interview with a natural charisma.

Virtual Interviews

Virtual Interviews are conducted in the comfort of your home. They are usually done via Zoom or Microsoft Teams.

Once you have booked a slot for your interview, you will be sent an invite nearer to the time of your interview with instructions, interview panel member names and a Microsoft Teams link to join the interview on the scheduled day and time.

For this type of Civil Service Interview, it is important to check your tech is all working; for example, you need to check if you can sign into Zoom or Microsoft Teams and that you can switch on the toggles for the Camera and Microphone when you click on the Teams link. If they aren't working, try restarting your laptop/computer, and hopefully, it will start working again.

Another good practice would be to set up a Microsoft Teams call with a friend or a family relative and get them to check they can hear and see you all fine.

Pre-Recorded Interviews

Pre-Recorded interviews are done on an online platform which the Recruitment Team set up with pre-recorded questions. You are required to record your responses to those questions and submit them when you go through each question.

It is good practice to prepare answers to common interview questions by recording yourself for a few minutes for each question. To get a flavour of the type of questions you may be asked at a pre-recorded interview, have a look at the job specification, more specifically, the Essential Criteria and Key Responsibilities. This will help you grasp an understanding of the areas of focus in the pre-recorded interview, so you feel more prepared for any questions that may come your way.

Format for Civil Service Interviews

Depending on the Civil Service Department and the role you have applied for, the format for Civil Service Interviews tends to vary. For example, if you have applied for a more analytical role such as a Data Analyst, you may be asked a series of Technical Questions to demonstrate the **Technical** element of the Success Profile Framework and may possibly have to deliver a presentation around your Research and Findings. Whereas, if you applied for a Diary Manager/PA role, you may be assessed on the **Experience** element of the

Success Profile Framework. It will test your ability to draft responses clearly and professionally through a Written exercise.

However, the standard format for Civil Service Interviews tends to follow something like this (this differs Department to Department depending on role and what they are looking for):

Introduction from Interview Panel Members – Panel Members will introduce themselves to you and a little about the role they play in the team.

What the Role Entails – The Lead Interviewer will briefly go into the specific details of the role you've applied for.

Icebreaker Question – The Lead Interviewer will ask an icebreaker question to make you feel comfortable and relaxed throughout the process to break the ice that is welling up within you. An example of an icebreaker question would be **'What interested you in applying for this role?'** or **'What do you enjoy doing outside work?'**

Behavioural Questions – Panel Members will take turns in asking you a set of Behavioural Questions in relation to the Civil Service Behaviours relevant to the role.

Strengths Questions – Panel Members will ask a set of Strengths Questions which require you to think outside the box and give immediate, natural responses to Strengths Questions linked to Behaviours.

Interview Close – Lead Interviewer will close the interview and open the floor for any questions you may have regarding the role, career progression, research you have done on the company, etc.

10 Interview Strategies which worked for me

Having completed dozens of Civil Service Interviews from **AO-SEO** levels, I can confidently say I have had a fair share in terms of how to prepare for Civil Service Interviews. I have constantly found myself testing the waters surrounding interview strategies and seeing what kept me afloat in the waters without the need to drown in heavy waters (rigid preparation for interviews).

In this section, we will delve into 10 interview strategies which worked for me through some exercises and visuals to aid you.

Interview Strategy Exercise 1:

Personal Achievements

For this first Interview Strategy Exercise, we will explore everything about you and what you can bring to the team. This is vital when sitting a Civil Service Job Interview as the Interview Panel Members would like to understand what makes you tick and how you bring your unique qualities into a role. That is the key which will unlock their mind to the possibility of a candidate who has no direct experience for the role; however, what the candidate will have is the passion, aura, and drive to confidently talk about what they have achieved and how they have achieved what they did.

To help you get started with this first Exercise, I would like you to draw a bubble big enough to write '**Personal Achievements**' in it. As said before, this is about you and your offerings to the potential team you see yourself working with.

Coming out of the bubble you've drawn will be multiple arrows to showcase all the many things you have achieved in the last 3 years or so. We wouldn't want to go too far back with your personal achievements, as it is important to remember what you say in the interview needs to be recent and relevant. With your personal achievements, celebrate them as much as possible because you've achieved them with your input, which then resulted in an output (end product). Thinking this way will help you capture greater achievements you never thought you'd have achieved. In order to help you celebrate your personal achievements, let me open up my biggest personal achievement which was when I was working as an Admin Manager for the Probation Service. I compiled a 49-page Court Pack to support Case Administrators with Court Processes and enable the effective delivery of important Court Reports. For this personal achievement, I was given a reward and recognition with £100 worth of vouchers to spend on whatever I wanted – food, leisure, you name it.

Interview Strategy Exercise 2:
Research Homework

In this second Interview Strategy Exercise, we will be going back to our school days where we had to do our homework for every subject area regardless of whether we were bothered to complete it or not. This homework is no different. It's a Research homework. In order for you to understand the department's ethos, objectives, and culture, you do need to conduct thorough research. It will likely give you a clue as to whether the department you want to work for is aligned with your objectives or not.

So, to get you started, you must trust Google as your Buddy for the research you are about to conduct. In the Search Bar, type in the Government Department you will be interviewed by, and then always go for OFFICIAL websites like Gov.uk as they are authentic and reliable. Now, scroll through the Department's page and identify sections you will need. The sections you will definitely need are 'what they do', 'latest publications', and 'about us'. Once you have this information, you can come up with interview questions for the panel members, exercising your knowledge and research into the role by aligning it with the responsibilities listed in the job description. To put this into context for you, when I had a HEO Graded Job Interview for the Department for Transport for a Rail Data Analyst role, I ensured my research was relevant and specific to the role I was being interviewed for by viewing the Department for Transport Gov Publication Page with Statistics on Rail Timetables. This supported me in posing a question to the interview panel members on whether this work would be something I'd be doing. I shared Rail statistics to show my efforts in the research and passion for the role in that Department. They remembered me as someone who's done their Homework properly for once and ended up appreciating my efforts in the Research by adding it to the Interview Feedback.

Interview Strategy Exercise 3:
Behaviour Mind Map

In this third Interview Strategy Exercise, we will help you bring out the best Behaviours you can use for your interviews. A visual way of planning out which Behaviours would be deemed appropriate for an interview is by creating a Behaviour Mind Map. Let's get practical now – so what I would like you to do is grab a piece of paper and pen and draw a bubble in the middle which says 'Behaviours'. Going back to the drawing board – get your initial ideas down of what you have done in your previous roles and current role and identify the impact you made for the wider team. Then we will pull out the Success Profile Framework, refer to the grade the Interview is for and check to see if there's a match between the two. If there is a match and it's aligned, we extend the bubble with arrows for the Behaviours you will be assessed in the Interview and use the initial ideas to create quick and easy bullet points to convey the impactful stuff you've done in line with the Behaviours. Try to aim for two examples for each. Why? You may ask me. It's because when asked an interview question and you're like, 'oops, this isn't going to go down well' as it doesn't align with the example you were going to deliver, it can really set you off if you don't have a back-up to be able to tweak in response to the interview question posed to you. The format I would follow for the Behaviours Map is as follows:

1. **Brief context of your example – What is it about? What have you set yourself to achieve with it?**

2. **Bullet-pointed actions – this way it will be easier to follow through personally what you've done and how you achieved what you had to achieve.**
3. **Impact – what impact did you create through your actions? How did you fulfil the requirements of the behaviour through this impact?**

This will help fuel your idea spectrum, but to give you some context on how I have found suitable Behavioural Examples for my Civil Service Interviews, when I'm looking for inspiration for the Interview, I look at my Achievements Log, which I record every time a personal/professional milestone is achieved and align the examples to the Success Profile Criteria by sitting down and really thinking about how linked they are with the criteria for the Behaviours. One way I looked at this was, say, you're working on a big project; it could be developing a file structure plan for an information storage system. And, you could say it has a vision of 10 years where its purpose is for wider stakeholders in the organisation to use this file structure plan to navigate the information storage system within the 10 years. This type of example would be linked to 'Seeing the Big Picture' as you are developing this project to help others see the bigger picture in how it will have a positive impact on the delivery of work across the 10-year period, despite the consequences it can have if this process is not in place and managed appropriately.

Interview Strategy Exercise 4:
Aligning your Strengths with Civil Service Strengths

There's still the question of whether one should practice Strength-Based Questions for a Civil Service Interview. They are looking for your natural responses and how you think on the spot whilst being thrown multiple questions to showcase your strengths. In my opinion, I would still say PRACTICE! And in this exercise, I will show you exactly how you can PRACTICE!

As you may be familiar with the fact that for the Behaviours, you have a Civil Service Success Profile Behaviours PDF doc to understand what they're exactly looking for in your Behavioural Examples. Well, there is something similar called the 'Civil Service Strengths Dictionary'. The Civil Service Strengths Dictionary has a list of all the Strengths you can be assessed in any Civil Service Job Interview you go for. The good thing about it is it clearly tells you what each Strength is about and which Strengths go with the Behaviours.

For this exercise, I would like you to search 'Civil Service Strengths Dictionary' on Google or any Search Engine, click on the Gov Official link, open the file and scroll all the way down. Do you see the Strengths linked to the nine Behaviours? I want you to reflect on your achievements and strengths attached to them. Spend an hour if you need it to be able to understand your strengths – looking at the why, you will know how you acquired the strengths and the impact created from the strengths. And now, link them to the Civil Service Strengths and develop key examples of how you see your strengths in correlation with them, showing impact from your actions and the role you played, **NOT** what your team has done and the roles they played. Remember the emphasis is on **YOUR** actions and what you did; leave aside their actions when answering the Strengths-Based Questions in a Civil Service Job Interview.

Interview Strategy Exercise 5:
S.T.A.R Map

Do you sometimes find yourself waffling when you're answering a competency-based interview question, almost as if you lose the flow in your example?

In this Interview Strategy Exercise, I will make sure that your waffling stops through a powerful strategy I invented whilst undergoing my Interview Preparations for Civil Service Interviews. This Strategy is called the 'S.T.A.R Map'.

Get a blank piece of paper and tilt it so you're working on a landscape format.

Now going across the paper, write four letters spaced out and separated from one another: S, T, A and R. Once you have done that, go horizontal and have two bullet points for S, one bullet point for T, four bullet points for A and two bullet points for R. Notice that the four letters I have provided you with makeup what we use to give our answers to competency-based interview questions? The STAR method. Situation, Task, Action, and Result. However, by instilling this methodology in a creative way, you're able to entice the interview panel members with the context of your situation, addressing the underlying issue at hand, and explaining what your objective was, Or rather, your responsibility, followed by detailed actions on how you went about tackling the issue and finished with a compelling result your actions led to. The bullet points I've asked you to add in for each letter will help you follow the STAR methodology more concisely, especially when you get stuck midway answering an Interview Question and need a prompt to get you on track to complete your response to the maximum capacity.

Here's an example of a S.T.A.R Map I did for the Making Effective Decision Behaviour to bring this exercise to life. It gives you an idea of how to tackle yours in a way which works for you:

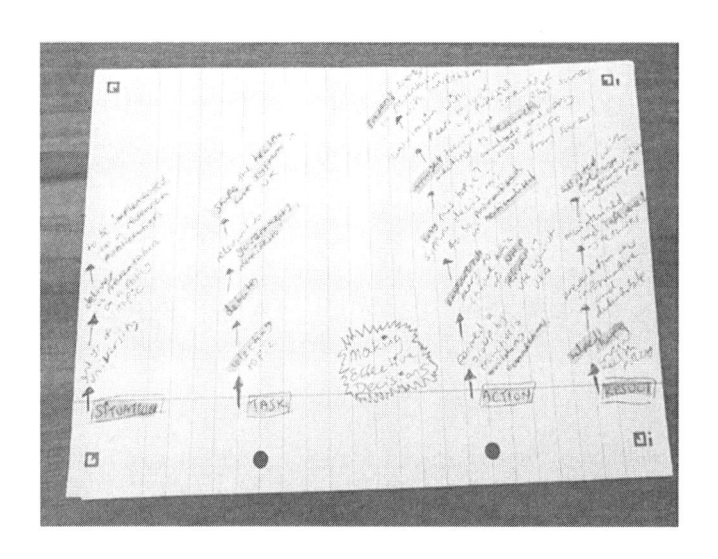

Interview Strategy Exercise 6:

Share your Story with someone – Recall and Retain Method

One other Interview Strategy which I found to be very effective is the 'Share your story with someone' method. It is a method used to help recall the information multiple times and retain it, so when your Interview Day is drawing near, you will be able to execute the delivery of your responses through a natural yet consistent flow to them. In my childhood, I remember watching a show on CBBC where someone would share a story to help us follow along and grasp the key moments and the moral of the story. Well, this Interview Strategy Exercise is no different. It's the exact same formula, but instead of sharing a story with a huge audience watching through a TV screen, you do it with a friend or relative on a Zoom Call or a Phone Call. The minimum time you need to make this work is 30 minutes, talking about different scenarios, the impact you created in each, and what it meant for the wider team in your department/organisation. Talking freely about it to someone allows you to remember your story and gets the person on the receiving end to observe how you execute your story. Because let's face it, you want to be your unique, true self throughout the Interview process. It is through this method that you can really give a compelling story of your experiences with an enthusiastic tone.

Interview Strategy Exercise 7:
Video Record yourself and Identify your Weak Points

For this Interview Strategy Exercise, we will teach you how to deliver in a Civil Service Interview with confidence, with no sign of nerves crawling around your mind. But this may seem cringe to you, I don't know, but have you considered video recording yourself how you would potentially answer typical Interview Questions? It is definitely a great way to see how you would ultimately present yourself to the Interview Panel. You can record yourself using a webcam camera, your phone camera (with a mini tripod to stabilise it) or an actual camera – however you want to record yourself practising with. Pace yourself through a timer and play the video to identify any weak points e.g., how you come across when answering the interview questions, your body language plays a huge part in verbal communication which we will look at in the 9th Interview Strategy Exercise.

Interview Strategy Exercise 8:
Spark an Initial Conversation with the Lead Interviewer (Interview Panel Chair)

Another Effective Strategy I found super helpful is being able to resonate with the Lead Interviewer through an open conversation from the get-go, as you click 'Join Meeting' in a Video Interview Meeting or shake hands with them in the 'In Person Interview'. It's the Interview Experience that counts, so let's make it worthwhile through this Interview Strategy Exercise, shall we?

Right! This may be daunting at first. I do sense those nerves of yours have skyrocketed at the sight of the word 'Job Interview'. Nothing for you to worry about, so don't fret. To tap into an inspiring conversation with the Lead Interviewer, you've got to stalk them on LinkedIn first; understand their background, how they are as well as some research into the team. If you cannot find them on LinkedIn, I'd advise from a personal standpoint to set up a one-to-one call prior to the interview to explore what they are about. You could take it further in the opening conversation during the Civil Service Interview. Remember, not to be dull in your approach by asking them how the weather looks in the area they're living in. Rather, bring a live atmosphere into an unpleasant interview environment by asking questions based on your research around them. This will highlight and reinforce that you really appreciate the work they do. You could perhaps ask them about what motivated them to make the career changes they did and the challenges they had to overcome in doing so. Or you could ask them what inspired them to work in the field they are in now, coming from X educational background.

Be yourself, conduct yourself with authenticity and openness, be professional and align your passions and enthusiasm with the Civil Service Core Values and the Department's Ethos. This will bring more authentic, honest and inspiring conversations with the Lead Interviewer, as you've got to remember they have the final say on who gets the job, so impress them, okay?

Interview Strategy Exercise 9:

Mirror your Reflection of Body Language, Posture and Facial Expression

Sometimes, it can be how we present ourselves when speaking to the Interview Panel Members which can determine how the interview experience goes. The most effective way of carrying yourself confidently in a Civil Service Interview, virtually or not, is to look in the mirror, practice talking about anything to judge yourself on how you are communicating. You have to mirror your true, natural self with positive body language, posture and facial expression. This is a confidence booster to help you naturally give effective and enthused responses in a Civil Service Interview.

Interview Strategy Exercise 10:
The Art of Articulacy

With this Interview Strategy Exercise, not only will you understand how to deliver the art of eloquent speech in a Civil Service Interview, you will be able to fathom how to give effective answers in a very concise and clear way.

So, let's dig into this a little bit further, shall we? When asked a difficult Civil Service Behaviour Question, your mind can go blank at the sight of hearing it. It can seem demoralising, but it really isn't. I can assure you if you strike the right balance using the Articulation of Thoughts, you will be fine, I promise!

How does one use Articulacy in a Civil Service Interview? Great question, fellow reader. Well, you see, when being asked an Interview Question, your reaction rate should not be as fast as a heartbeat. It needs to be just right, meaning it ought to be moderate – not too fast of a response and not too slow either. Just moderate. If the question is not clear to you, ask them to clarify what they meant and they will rephrase the question differently. This allows you to buy some time to collate your thoughts and go over your mind bank of examples for the behaviours they're assessing you on. Giving yourself a few seconds to spare will act as a prompt to help you deliver a more relevant example from your past job experiences, making your response to the interview question subtle, straight to the point, and behaviour-centric as well as going through a coherent structure.

Common Civil Service Interview Questions and Pointers to help you

Here are several common Civil Service Interview Questions which you may likely be asked for varying grades and Behaviours as well as a few pointers to help you understand the questions better, ensuring you ace that Civil Service Interview of yours.

Administrative Officer Level:
Managing a Quality Service

- Can you tell us a time when you had to deliver excellent customer service to someone?

Pointers to help you

- Think about a time when you were working in Retail. On the shop floor, you had to leave what you were doing, e.g. replenishing the stock of goods when a customer approached you for assistance. With a smile on your face and a positive attitude, you went out of your way to help them with their query. You listened to their query attentively, showcasing your ability to understand their needs and ask. This helped identify and address any issues the customer may have. You ensured excellent customer service was being delivered by taking your time to help the customer locate the product they're looking for, and if the product was not available in stock; you would work around it and find a solution by checking stock availability on the system. See if it can be delivered the next day. This ensures a quality service is maintained and your efforts of supporting the customer are recognised.

- Another way to think about this question is when one is working in a Call Centre. In a Call Centre, you're sat at a desk with numerous calls coming through. You have to show your resilience, positivity, and calm attitude in dealing with calls professionally. To help ascertain the client's needs and expectations, you would ask them a set of questions to gauge what they are calling for and how you may be able to assist them with their issues. You would try your very best in dealing with the client's concerns first. If this isn't possible and is proved to be difficult, you will ask for support from someone Senior to help rectify the situation. This still fulfils the purpose of managing a quality service for clients and ensures the clients are the heart of everything you do in a customer-focused environment.

Developing Self and Others

- Tell me about a time when you accepted feedback from others about your ways of learning at work. How did you improve your professional development at work and develop other colleagues in the process?

Pointers to help you

- Think about a time when you joined as a new starter and preferred to apply your ways of learning at work; however, colleagues suggested that you remain open to a different approach to how you learn in this new working environment. This is where you need to show your willingness to learn new things by understanding the processes and taking on extra e-learning to familiarise yourself with different areas of work, adopt a new approach, but still think creatively on how you can apply existing methods of learning. Through this professional development, you will be in the position to support other colleagues in the process, reminding them of the benefits of undertaking mandatory e-learning modules and extra e-learning according to their interests and passion for developing both personal and professional development areas.

Working Together

- Tell me about a time when you worked collaboratively in a team and how you built a supportive relationship with your colleagues.

Pointers to help you

- Think about a time when you took part in some form of volunteering and how you contributed towards the success of others. It could be volunteering as a

Student Ambassador at your University. You had to work collaboratively with others by asking questions if unsure of how to guide and signpost first-year and second-year students to the relevant Departments and other services such as Finance and Student Enquiries. This showcases you're able to work with others. You also had to interact with other Student Ambassadors to understand a little bit about what they are studying and how they are finding it to build that supportive relationship with your peers because you're all on the same journey in terms of studying and hopefully graduating together.

- The other way to think about this question is, say one is volunteering for a charitable organisation (taking Oxfam as an example). Their role is to help alleviate poverty by supporting the cause through volunteering to maintain the stock of clothes and other products which had been taken into the shop for donation. They engage and communicate with other volunteers to raise money to support a cause that is close to their heart. The money that is made in Oxfam goes towards an important cause to help the needy. This is the quality of service managed by getting involved and being a part of something that will make a significant difference in the community. This is how a supportive team can ensure the best interests of the people in the community by giving back to it through charitable causes and aligning their volunteering work to Oxfam's vision: Being able to alleviate poverty around the world.

Changing and Improving

- Tell me about a time when you suggested a change in the workplace and how you got others on board with the change.

Pointers to help you

- Think about a time when you were working in your previous role and noticed a particular process was long-winded. How did you address this problem to seniors, explaining the need for this process to be streamlined? Bringing your own perspective on the idea for change will help others see the need for change.
- Another way you can think about this question is, let's say, in an office environment, you have noticed that all this time records have been paper-based; colleagues have been reluctant to move onto digital storage (i.e., kept on SharePoint or a shared drive) in case a fire breaks out. It is important to have a backup for important company documentation to prevent any loss of work. That allows you to carry out your work effectively in the organisation.

Executive Officer Level:
Communicating & Influencing

- Tell me about a time when you used a range of communication methods to communicate an important message to someone.

Pointers to help you

- Think about a time when you used written communication to communicate something important to a member of your team. For example, you could write an email to someone, sharing important agenda items, or more importantly, you could be drafting the minutes for a team meeting, and it needs to be circulated widely to relevant people who need to know if there are any actions to consider. Also think about other ways you'd communicate an important message such as briefing the team verbally on key changes which will come into the organisation, affecting everyone in the areas of work.

Delivering at Pace

- Tell me about a time when you had to deliver a piece of project through a tight deadline. How did you ensure you made time for this project to become a success?

Pointers to help you

- You could think about a last-minute project (deadline being the next few days) which was assigned to you by your manager and how you had to prioritise this alongside your other tasks. This would be through understanding the project assignment, what was expected of you and working with other stakeholders in the wider team to ensure the successful delivery of this project. A more effective way of tackling a last-minute piece of project is by finding out the key information you need and the most important documents you need to collate as part of the project. This will ensure relevance in the project and will see through its success.

Managing a Quality Service

- Can you tell me a time when you had to deliver an excellent service to end users? Think about the service you provided in a retail environment or office environment.

Pointers to help you

- In a Retail Context, you could think about how you value a Customer's time when providing a service to them, understanding the urgency they may have, for example, when they are catching a train to their workplace. So, you need to ensure you are being attentive to their needs and providing exactly what

they are looking for, ensuring customer satisfaction in the whole process.
- In an Admin Context, you could think about how you add value to other stakeholders to deliver a service on the front-line. This could be through the way you complete administrative tasks, which can be made easier for all stakeholders and potentially the end users.

Making Effective Decisions

- Tell me about a time when you used various sources to form an effective decision.

Pointers to help you

- You could use an example from college if it's been a couple of years since, where for your A Levels/BTEC, you had to undertake Coursework Assignments, which required you to look at primary and secondary sources of information. Using the various sources of information, you had to form an effective decision as to which parts would be relevant in forming your arguments and answering the question that is posed.
- In a University Context, you have to undertake a Research Project or a Dissertation/Thesis on a particular topic. This requires you to pick a topic for your Research Paper, so your Critical Thinking and Articulacy are needed to support your decision. You would have to look at Case Studies and the Content from your University Lectures and Seminars to base

your decision. Sometimes, you may need to do a consensus where you gather opinions from the public on the topic to make well-informed arguments to back up your idea for the thesis.

Changing & Improving

- Tell me about a time when you had to change an existing process. What did you do? How did you go about the change?

Pointers to help you

- Think about when you noticed others in the team were experiencing difficulties with a system and it has been affecting their ability to do their work. What could you have done to streamline the system? You could put in place a backup for important documents if they ever get lost on the server through a network problem. This will exercise your creative ingenuity in solving a problem for the wider organisation and improves how processes are running in a workplace.

Higher Executive Officer Level:
Communicating & Influencing

- Tell me about a time when you had to influence a senior official to go with your approach.

Pointers to help you

- Think about a piece of work you have done which received positive feedback and the go-ahead for implementation. Use this as one of the ways to get someone's buy-in. To put this into perspective, when I used to work as an Administrative Officer for the Probation Service, I built new experience in devising training materials on Administrative Processes for Case Administrators to effectively perform their roles and support the Probation Practitioners. I received positive feedback from my manager, administrators I used to work with and the Head of Probation Delivery Unit. I used this as a foundation for my story to influence a senior official when I moved into a new role.

Leadership

- Can you give us a time when you had to motivate your team to engage with the work? How did you ensure you set the direction for the team in order to achieve optimal results?

Pointers to help you

- When leading a team, think about the needs of colleagues and how you got them on board. To boost team morale for colleagues to engage with the work, you can support them by getting them to celebrate their wins so far and realise their potential. Think

about how you made colleagues feel included by respecting their cultural differences and etiquette. This will increase the serotonin of your colleagues as they are being appreciated and valued. This in turn boosts team morale and allows them to continue doing the most in the work that they do.
- Think about a time when you had to make the organisational goals clearer for your team and highlighted the benefits of achieving these goals e.g., executing a plan to track their progress and reviewing it now and then.

Making Effective Decisions

- Can you tell us a time when you had to use analysis to help inform your decision-making? How did you come to an effective decision for the team?

Pointers to help you

- There are numerous ways to look at this. Still, one effective way you can look at this is by understanding the data you used for your analysis, more specifically, dig into the 'why?', why was it essential for you to use this data to help inform your decision?
- When using analysis to inform your decision-making, you may have to evaluate the data in terms of its application to the topic, how accurate it is in providing the information needed to make an effective decision and the importance to the topic at hand.

Delivering at Pace

- Tell me a time when you had to deliver a challenging project on time. How did you manage multiple work streams whilst doing so?

Pointers to help you

- Think about when you had to complete a complex task with a tight deadline. How do you normally set aside time to complete the task alongside other important commitments? This is where you need to block out some time to dedicate towards this very complex task and set yourself reminders so you stay focused on the quality of the project with due diligence.

Working Together

- Tell me about a time when you instilled team spirit within your team to achieve a common goal in the organisation.

Pointers to help you

- To instil team spirit, you could acknowledge their efforts in the team by recognising them through a reward scheme, raises, and your ongoing support. It also helps when you remind them of the goal in the organisation from time to time and provide them with a helping hand on what they can do at the workplace to help achieve the common goal.

Senior Executive Officer Level:
Seeing the Big Picture

- Can you tell me how you had to see the big picture? What factors did you take into consideration when achieving the immediate outcome?

Pointers to help you

- Think about what the vision for your organisation is. It could be a short-term objective or it can span for years, thus becoming a long-term objective. When I was an Admin Manager for the Probation Service, our vision was to deliver services to Probation Users which would benefit them in the long run in the community, so they do not re-offend and go back to their old ways. I reflected on this vision and thought about how my role fits in with this vision. I thought to myself, 'What can I do better in my role to achieve this vision?'. So, an eureka moment came about where rather than doing the tedious admin work, I put my creative thinking hat on and started looking at the notes I made on each admin process. Using the notes I made, I opened up Microsoft Word and began drafting guides for each process. This helped others in the wider team in being proactive with the work and seeing that the work they're producing is amounted to something big – it is making a difference to how services are being facilitated and provided to Probation users in the Probation Service to protect the public.

Making Effective Decisions

- Tell me about a time when you had to consider multiple options when making a difficult decision for the team

Pointers to help you

- Think about a time when you used Risk Analysis to look at possible options when tackling a difficult decision for the team. One way I see it is when it's about risk, it can focus on the SWOT Framework. If you break it down, it identifies key areas of a risk when making a difficult decision. To better manage a risk, you have to dig into the strengths of the team as a whole. Find out what each individual is good at. Then you take another layer which is 'weaknesses'. find areas of improvement in the team to mitigate the risk when making big decisions for the organisation. Then, you have the 'opportunities' to control the risk to prevent the decision going haywire. And finally, threats. What type of threats are posed to the wider team if inaccurate and poor decision making is devised?

Communicating & Influencing

- Can you tell me a time when you had to communicate with a range of stakeholders, ensuring you were understood through your communication?

Pointers to help you

- Think about when you had to communicate with a range of people in various teams. Let's set an example to help you understand what I mean. In Retail, you're not only conversing with colleagues in the ales department. In fact, you're communicating with people in other departments such as the merchandising department to find out the stock availability of a product for a customer who's looking specifically for something to go with the occasion. And, you also have to communicate with your Senior Managers to find out about new stock arrivals coming into the store and how to prepare for the new stock. Obviously, you would have to engage in meetings to come up with a marketing strategy to ensure new stock is laid out correctly in each area of the store. You would make sure your communication is understood by voicing your ideas in a way where your tone of language is clear to the audience whilst respecting the opinions of others in the team.

Civil Service Interviews – What you need to do vs What you should not do

What you need to do vs What you should not do - Civil Service Interviews

Do's

- Pause when a question is asked to help reflect on what they have asked you to give a response to
- Listen attentively to the question asked and analyse the keywords in the question to help structure your example more coherently and clearly - this helps to avoid waffling and being irrelevant in your examples
- Have water on the side to keep yourself hydrated as speaking a lot can make your lips and throat dry
- Light exercises to boost your confidence in yourself - have that belief in yourself that you can storm through the interview with great examples
- Sleep early - a healthy habit which will help reap results on the day of your interview
- Ask questions based on the role and opportunities available. Let your passion for the role shine through and demonstrate the research you've done to showcase your knowledge around a specific topic

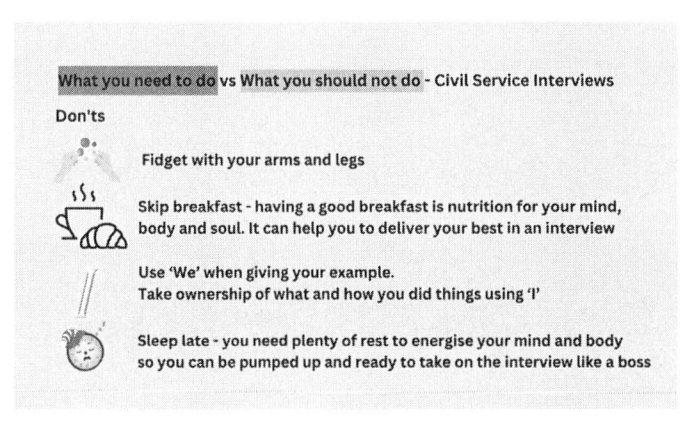

What you need to do vs What you should not do - Civil Service Interviews

Don'ts

- Fidget with your arms and legs
- Skip breakfast - having a good breakfast is nutrition for your mind, body and soul. It can help you to deliver your best in an interview
- Use 'We' when giving your example. Take ownership of what and how you did things using 'I'
- Sleep late - you need plenty of rest to energise your mind and body so you can be pumped up and ready to take on the interview like a boss

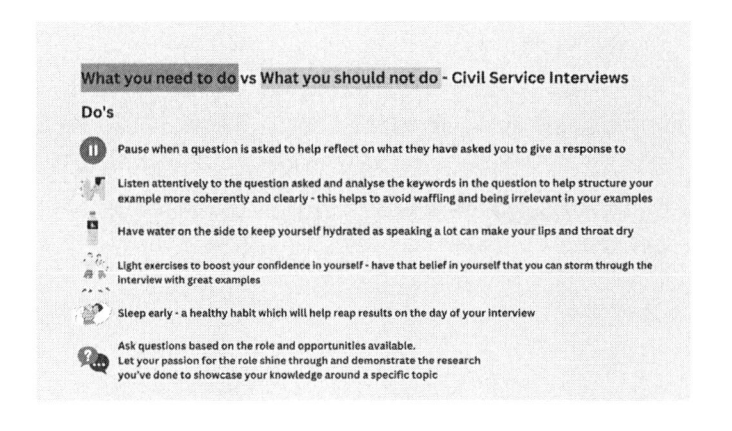

Key Takeaway Gems from this Chapter:

1. **S.T.A.R Map** is one of many interview strategies which helps you break down the STAR methodology and use it easily as brief notes for a Civil Service Interview.

2. Celebrate your achievements and own the things you have done. We easily get into a habit where we credit others for the work but do not credit ourselves in the process.
3. There are three types of Civil Service Interviews; Face-to-Face, Pre-Recorded, and Virtual.
4. There is a form of Art in attracting the attention of the Interview Panel Chair.

Concluding Remarks

In conclusion, Civil Service is a rewarding Career; one which opens doors of opportunities for those who aspire to get into the many fields. It certainly paved the way for me in navigating my career, but I hope it has taught you that you may not land in your desired Career right now, but you will definitely get there through your passion, dedication, patience, and perseverance.

When I graduated from university, like you may have, it is fair to say that I was confused about which career direction to take. I'm pretty sure we all felt it at that stage and had the urge to get into whatever role we could find and where our luck would strike a pot of gold. Never would I have thought about working for the Civil Service; in fact, I saw myself working for corporate investment banks, doing longer hours and overtime, tiring my eyes out. It is absolutely okay to feel like that, because truly, there was a lack of resources especially when it came to navigating careers within the Civil Service and having someone to guide you through the whole process.

By now, having reached the end of this book, I hope you have been educated well through interesting lessons regarding the introduction to what the Civil Service is really about, the routes you can take, the benefits of working for the Civil Service, the importance of transferable experiences and applying strategies in the application process, and the interview process.

Let us now briefly summarise these chapters you have read to this end:

In Chapter 1, we looked at personal challenges one can possibly be faced with when you initially start the process of applying for the UK Civil Service. It can be a daunting experience, especially when there isn't much of a tailored guidance and support around.

In Chapter 2, we explored how imposter syndrome affects us all by limiting our potential and capabilities of going for that job we don't meet 100% of the criteria for. It is okay if you don't meet 100% of the criteria; there is always room for improvement as the Civil Service is a place to learn and develop your skills and a way for you to progress upwards. You can control the fears and anxiety of applying for big departments – it is a matter of how you overcome your doubts and allow positivity and optimism to shine right through you throughout the process.

In Chapter 3, we looked at the Civil Service Graded Structure and what it means to someone who's new to applying for the Civil Service or wants to progress within the Civil Service.

In Chapter 4, we took a look into the Civil Service Application Process through two cycles: Traditional Route where you apply on the Civil Service Jobs. And, the Fast

Stream Route where you apply on the Civil Service Fast Stream Site.

In Chapter 5, we explored transferable experiences required for applying to Civil Service Roles. It draws upon experiences in Retail, Admin, Content Creation, and Event Management and how they have relevance when applying for the Civil Service.

In Chapter 6, we looked at the wide range of benefits of working for the Civil Service and what other Civil Servants had to say about the perks of working in the Civil Service.

In Chapter 7, we explored the Civil Service Behaviours in-depth with practical exercises to aid you in thinking about the Behaviours. We came up with examples to link well with the Civil Service Success Profile Framework.

In Chapter 8, we looked at the types of a personal statement you may need to write, the structure it follows compared to a private sector personal statement, and ways you can write a compelling personal statement through practical exercises.

In Chapter 9, we explored the various types of Civil Service Interviews in different formats, what the process entails, how you can practice interview questions, and prepare for a Civil Service Interview through practical exercises.

References

Cabinet Office (2019) *Success Profiles: Civil Service Behaviours*. Available at:
https://assets.publishing.service.gov.uk/government/uploads/system/uploads/attachment_data/file/717275/CS_Behaviours_2018.pdf (Accessed: 19/08/2023).

Cabinet Office (2019) *Success Profiles: Civil Service Strengths Dictionary*. Available at:
https://assets.publishing.service.gov.uk/government/uploads/system/uploads/attachment_data/file/717274/CS_Strengths_2018.pdf (Accessed: 19/08/2023).

Cabinet Office (2021) *Civil Service Fast Stream*. Available at:
https://www.faststream.gov.uk/index.html (Accessed: 19/08/2023).